Design Guidelines for a Monitoring Environment Concerning Distributed Real-Time Systems

— As Means for Achieving Dependability Control through Dynamic Adaption of Distributed Real-Time Target Systems Under Operation

Design Guidelines for a Monitoring Environment Concerning Distributed Real-Time Systems

— As Means for Achieving Dependability Control through Dynamic Adaption of Distributed Real-Time Target Systems Under Operation

by
Aida Omerovic

tapir academic press

© Tapir Academic Press, Trondheim 2004

ISBN 82-519-1931-2

This publication may not be reproduced, stored in a retrieval system or transmitted in any form or by any means; electronic, electrostatic, magnetic tape, mechanical, photo-copying, recording or otherwise, without permission.

Layout: The author
Printed by Tapir Uttrykk
Binding: Grafisk Produksjonsservice AS

Tapir Academic Press
N–7005 TRONDHEIM
Tel.:   + 47 73 59 32 10
Fax: + 47 73 59 32 04
E-mail: forlag@tapir.no
www.tapirforlag.no

Abstract

The book offers a an innovative approach and deduces a framework for monitoring dependability characteristics. Dependability characteristics, encompassing both the functional and the non-functional requirements, are preserved by providing an architecture for dynamic adaption of a distributed target system by the monitoring environment.

It summarises the relevant techniques and theories, offers a completely new approach, includes an in-depth qualitative and quantitative analysis and proposes a holistic solution. It is applicable in real-time (distributed) systems of all sizes and requirements. The results represent a significant contribution to the subject and expert groups (industry, educational institutions) in both electrical engineering and computer sciences will benefit from the contents of the book. It is well applicable both as a surway, a handbook, a problem solving guide, or as a review of author's latest achievements and solution proposals. The solutions proposed are unique in its nature, highly needed and desired in many branches of the industry, well documented, structured, throughtfully analysed, as well as technically implementable and economically justifiable, due to the significant benefits (as seen from all the stakeholders' viewpoints) and limited costs.

It is discussed how to reveal, define, quantify, measure, analyze, design, implement, test, monitor and enhance dependability requirements of a distributed system with real-time constraints. An overview of the tools and methodologies applicable has been given and an alternative method for ensuring continuous fulfillment of system requirements, proposed. It is presented how the requirements can be achieved, verified and controlled throughout the system life-cycle stages, and what tools and methodologies are applicable under different constraints and with maximized cost effectiveness.

The concept of system integrity is introduced and put in relation to dependability and risk. A risk analysis framework has been deduced and integrated with the main lines from the dependability and integrity approaches, giving a structured knowledge platform for training, pattern recognition and automated intervention of the monitoring environment.

Separate chapters are devoted to the most critical issues of real-time and distributed systems, relating them to the rest of the study, and, when appropriate, proposing the methods of addressing them.

The main contribution comes from the active monitoring approach, which takes advantage of the main achievements from the earlier stages of the study, thus representing a mechanism for continuous dependability requirements control and verification during system operation. The deduced real-time monitoring environment measures the degree of requirements fulfillment, relates it to the pre-defined, measurable system-level expectations and dynamically adapts the system, based on quality metrics, risk analysis, cost evaluation, control theory, neural networks, data acquisition and system knowledge management.

The result is a self-controlled system, evolvable over time. Overall architecture of the monitoring environment is developed, along with lower-level design of some critical modules, implementational issues discussed and general design guidelines proposed.

The utility of some of the main ideas has been verified through conducting interviews with key system developers and researchers, as well as an expert in artificial intelligence.

As a result, the approach proposes a new method for defining dependability at the earliest stages of a system life-cycle, followed by implementing, controlling and improving the requirements by an integrated application of the results obtained and inclusion of a separate monitoring environment.

Thus, the framework provides a multilevel specification mechanism to establish the preservation of system requirements. This ensures the correct functioning of system through adaptions at run time. Among the benefits are controlled access and coordinated resource sharing in accordance with service-level agreement policies, multi-stakeholder interest preservation, transparancy with respect to location, naming, performance etc., achievement of quality of service on demand, decentralization, seamless integration of resources and applications, as well as increased predictability.

Preface

This text is originally a thesis, submitted in fulfillment of the requirements of the compulsory final (project) course towards the degree Master of Science in Engineering Cybernetics at NTNU - Norwegian University of Science and Technology, Trondheim, Norway. The study has been conducted at NTNU over a period of five months, from January 2002 until June 2002. The topic is inspired by and partly a continuation of the author's previous study under the title "An Integrated Approach to Dependability of Real-Time Telecommunications Applications Systems", conducted at SERC - Software Engineering Research Centre at RMIT - Royal Melbourne Institute of Technology, Melbourne, Australia, over a period of five months, from June until November 2001.

The intended audience is broad: real time and distributed systems scientists and developers, software engineers, students, quality assurance managers, contractors, users, service providers and all those searching for an alternative approach to handling and ensuring automated control of fulfillment of system requirements. Moreover, those needing knowledge about methods to apply, under various circumstances, in regards to long lived projects with high dependability and integrity demands.

Many people deserve acknowledgment and I wish I could mention them all. I am indebted to my supervisor at NTNU, Professor Odd Pettersen for his support of the idea, encouragement and valuable comments during the entire course of my studies, particularly during the project-related part which has lasted for more than a year. My sincere thanks also go to my supervisor at SERC, Professor Fergus O'Brien and his group for introducing me into the topic of dependability and all the support I received during my stay at RMIT while conducting the above mentioned preceding project. I am greatly thankful to a group of people from Western Geco for their interest in the thesis, positive feedback and a fruitful cooperation. I have particularly benefited from the contact with Mr. Thorleiv Knutsen and his feedback, which I appreciate. My thanks also go to Mr. Espen Krogh from Prediktor AS for showing interest in the study and for supplying the valuable documentation. Mr. Pavel Petrovic's comments and suggestions in about the middle of the study helped verify the utility of the monitoring ideas and plan further work. There are a number of people at the department of Engineering Cybernetics who have frequently been available and helpful with all the kinds of administrative and technical support, which I appreciate. Last but definitely not least, a special thank goes to my friends and family for all their patience, never-ending encouragement and help along the way.
Thank you all, this thesis would never have been possible without your contributions.

Trondheim, June 2002
Aida Omerovic

Table of Contents

Chapter 1: Introduction 1
   1.1 Background 1
   1.2 Purpose 3
   1.3 Constraints 4
   1.4 Method 6
   1.5 Outline of the thesis 6

Chapter 2: Dependability framework 9
   2.1 Introduction 9
   2.2 History and the current achievements 10
   2.3 On the impairments to dependability 13
   2.4 Software aspects of dependability 15
   2.5 Towards a general definition of dependability 17
      2.5.1 Framework deduction 18
         2.5.1.1 Life-cycle stage categories 21
         2.5.1.2 Deduction of system dependability factors 23
         2.5.1.3 Deduction of system dependability criteria 37
         2.5.1.4 Deduction of criteria related metrics 42
         2.5.1.5 Overall dependability evaluation 46
         2.5.1.6 Requirements specification as a prerequisite 47
      2.5.2 A dependability cost-benefit model 48
         2.5.2.1 Cost of failures 50
      2.5.3 Total Quality Management 51
      2.5.4 The general methodology deduction 52
   2.6 Dependability achievement and measurement 55
      2.6.1 Dependability means 55
      2.6.2 Dependability control process 56
      2.6.3 Methods for dependability achievement 57
      2.6.4 Methods for dependability assessment 61
   2.7 Summary 64

Chapter 3: Risk analysis and treatment 65
   3.1 Introduction 65
   3.2 Integrity definition 65
      3.2.1 Integrity metrics deduction 67
         3.2.1.1 Component-based approach 67
         3.2.1.2 System-based approach 70
   3.3 Life-cycle risk analysis activities 72
   3.4 Statistical Process Control 73
   3.5 A risk and vulnerability analysis framework 74
   3.6 Guidelines for framework application 76
   3.7 Summary 77

Chapter 4: Real-time system considerations 78
   4.1 Introduction 78
   4.2 Real-time requirements 78
   4.3 Transactions and concurrency control 81
   4.4 Performance evaluation in parallel systems 82
      4.4.1 Performance observability 83
   4.5 Summary 84

Chapter 5: Distributed systems 85
   5.1 Introduction 85
   5.2 Main issues and characteristics 85
   5.3 Useful techniques 87
   5.4 Requirements on distributed systems 88
   5.5 Distributed databases 89
      5.5.1 Active database systems 90
      5.5.2 Requirements 90

5.6 Summary..........91

Chapter 6: A monitoring framework for distributed real-time systems..........92
  6.1 Introduction..........92
  6.2 Monitoring of distributed real-time programs..........93
  6.3 Run-time software monitoring..........94
  6.4 Control theory and neural networks in software monitoring..........97
  6.5 Monitor correctness..........102
  6.6 Testing within monitoring environment..........102
    6.6.1 Test data generation..........103
    6.6.2 Testing foci..........103
    6.6.3 Levels of testing..........104
    6.6.4 Testing system selections..........105
    6.6.5 Automation of the testing process..........106
  6.7 Using Erlang as a monitoring programming language..........110
  6.8 The cost of monitoring..........111
    6.8.1 Monitoring overhead..........111
  6.9 Run-time monitoring of dependability attributes..........113
    6.9.1 Enhancing the process of software development..........113
  6.10 General system monitoring guidelines..........114
  6.11 Real-time databases in intrusive monitoring..........116
  6.12 Further discussion on the benefits of monitoring..........119
  6.13 Maintenance..........121
  6.14 Integrity monitoring..........123
  6.15 Architecture proposal for a monitoring environment..........125
    6.15.1 Data acquisition..........127
    6.15.2 Event recognition..........127
    6.15.3 Data processing and system[62] training..........128
    6.15.4 Knowledge management..........129
    6.15.5 Data analysis..........130
    6.15.6 System diagnosis and pattern recognition..........131
    6.15.7 Action control and system intervention..........131
    6.15.8 Action verification..........133
    6.15.9 Implementational issues..........134
    6.15.10 Simulations and testing..........134
    6.15.11 Reporting facility..........135
    6.15.12 Further implementational issues..........136
    6.15.13 Further implementational issues..........140
    6.15.14 Timing budgets..........141
    6.15.15 Performance evaluation environment..........142
  6.16 Summary..........144

Chapter 7: Industrial experiences..........145
  7.1 Introduction..........145
  7.2 Western Geco..........145
    7.2.1 Requirements from the monitoring environment..........147
    7.2.2 Feedback on the presented monitoring environment architecture..........148
  7.3 Prediktor..........150
    7.3.1 APIS..........150
    7.3.2 Feedback on the presented monitoring environment..........150
  7.4 Department of Computer and Information Science, Intelligent Systems Group..........151
  7.5 Summary..........153

Chapter 8: Conclusions and further recommendations..........154
  8.1 Conclusions..........154
  8.2 Recommendations..........155

Bibliography..........157

  Appendix A: Elementary definitions..........A-1
  Appendix B: Erlang..........B-1
  Appendix C: Interview with Mr. Thorleiv Knutsen, WesternGeco..........C-1

Chapter 1: Introduction

*"Quality is never an accident;
it is always the result of intelligent effort."*
John Ruskin

As an increasing range of industries, users and society at large have a growing dependence upon software-based control systems, communication systems, their applications and services, the demands on such systems expand. Real-time systems are being assigned new application areas, resulting in larger criticality of the applications. The key characteristics of these systems are their complexity, large-scale distribution, inclusion of legacy and Commercial Off The Shelf (COTS) components, mobility and flexibility. The systems cover safety-, mission-, security- and business-critical systems, as well as a broad range of emerging application areas such as embedded systems in consumer goods, health support, personal communications, electronic commerce and transport. The novelty of the applications, the extensively deployed nature of new technologies and their common characteristics give rise to new types of problems and challenges to dependability technologies.

Dependability should be understood as encompassing the whole system life-cycle. The gap between dependability analysis and design models should be closed. A lot of current design tools, especially those for dependable software, are immature, and design processes rarely focus adequately on dependability aspects. Implicit here is the integration between functional and non-functional requirements.

1.1 Background

The thesis is motivated by, and partly a continuation of, the author's previously conducted research at SERC - Software Engineering Research Centre at RMIT (Royal Melbourne Institute of Technology) university, Melbourne, Australia. The project was submitted in fulfillment of requirements of the compulsory project course and discussed how to define, measure, analyze, test and enhance dependability requirements of a telecommunications applications system with real-time constraints. The main ideas were verified through a case study on a distributed telecommunications system.

While the dependability requirements of distributed real-time systems are expanding, there is currently no framework for defining and mapping these requirements into the system design and operation. Dependability requirement specifications need to be expanded to encompass all system resources in a manner that permits global, end-to-end assurance and clear bindings between requirement specifications during the different phases of system life cycle.

A method of controlling and achieving the dependability level is real-time monitoring, which measures the degree of requirements fulfillment, relates it to system-level expectations and manipulates the system if necessary.

One can distinguish between three main categories of analytic activities: static, dynamic and formal analysis. Static analysis is the analysis of the development phases[1] either manually or automatically.

Dynamic analysis techniques involve the execution of a product and analysis of its response to sets of input data to determine its validity and to detect errors. The behavioural properties of the system are also observed. Dynamic analysis is performed by testing, simulations and monitoring.

Formal methods involve rigorous mathematical techniques to specify, analyze and verify system requirements, design or code. Examples include metrics and specification languages.

The resulting monitoring environment presented in chapter 6 represents the a tool for understanding the methodology of the framework and evaluating its usefulness in practice.

---

1 Examples include requirements, design, code, testing and documentation.

1.2 Purpose

The above mentioned research project revealed a need for inclusion of the issues of distribution, real-time (databases), cost-effectiveness and correctness into the approach, as well as bringing further the ideas of control through monitoring by developing a monitoring framework and proposing design guidelines for a monitoring environment.

Monitoring, as defined in this study, was seen as the method of controlling system dependability and tracing the system characteristics back into the pre-defined, quantifyible requirements. It offered a solution to all the identified issues and a number of additional benefits, which all together easily justified the use of the framework. One could not only prove the fulfillment of the system requirements, but also vary and control the dependability levels in real time.

The idea is to enable dynamic adjustments of the target system under execution and by a self-evolving intelligent monitoring environment which would perform changes on the target system in real time and in accordance with the dependability requirements. The monitoring environment's operation would include measurements of the relevant parts of the system as rigorously specified in the requirements (described in the dependability framework), analysis and run-time modifications. The usage takes place under the operation but offers benefits to the entire development cycle, as well as future systems.

The framework provides a multilevel specification mechanism to establish the preservation of system requirements. This ensures the correct functioning of system through adaptions at run time. Among the benefits are controlled access and coordinated resource sharing in accordance with service-level agreement policies, multi-stakeholder interest preservarion, transparancy with respect to location, naming, performance etc., achievement of quality of service on demand, decentralization, seamless integration of resources and applications, increased predictability and so forth.

As such, the monitoring environment solves nearly all the issues of controlling system dependability. The question that arises, however, is the one of how realistic the approach is when it comes to implementation, overhead, costs and preserving the target system's functionalities. These are some of the issues intended to be solved by this study through proposing design guidelines for the monitoring environment.

The objective is:
- To conduct an investigation of the current achievements within the related topics, including system dependability achievement methods, real-time techniques, distributed systems, testing, monitoring approaches, programming language characteristics and hardware issues.
- To derive a meaning for "dependability" for a computer based system that can be defined, implemented, measured, tested and monitored and to discuss the methods for specification, measurement, control, achievement and enhancement throughout the system life-cycle.
- To derive a definition of integrity and deduce a risk framework encompassing the dependability and integrity analysis and achievement and serving as a knowledge platform.
- To discuss the issues of real-time system architecture, cost-efficiency, real-time databases, distribution, testing and verification.
- To develop design guidelines for a monitoring environment used for dependability enhancement and control through active surveillance and modification.

The primary hypothesis is two-fold:
- Dependability of real-time systems should be an integrated part of the development process and it can be defined, evaluated, observed, verified and controlled in real time.
- Continuous dependability monitoring can provide significant quality gains and guarantee continuous requirements fulfillment, without major degradation of user perceived performance.

1.3 Constraints

The study has been made with large distributed real-time systems in mind, although the general methodology will be applicable on most other types of control target systems. Due to time and space limitations, the relevant topics on which earlier research results or adequate theory has been found, are provided with references and in some cases briefly presented, if appropriate.

The nature of the thesis demands a wide-spanned approach and involves a considerable number of issues to be addressed. Having this in mind, the resulting monitoring framework offers a completely new approach to controlling system dependability and represents an extensive solution to the problem. Therefore, the complexity and extension of the monitoring environment have put limitations on how far in detail the design guidelines should be given in a generalized case.

An important requirement on the monitoring environment is that it is recommended to be designed in parallel with the target system, which puts limitations on possibilities of adding the monitoring environment to an already implemented target system.

The framework does not offer any design specification tools beyond the dependability metrics, although a convention on notation and some implementational issues would be desirable to achieve consistency and simplify reuse.

Emphasis has been put on the software aspects of the monitoring environment and the framework in general, and hardware-related approach has only been included when necessary.

Beyond feedback from industry professionals and experts, no verification of the monitoring approach has been carried out. Although such a verification is not an objective of the thesis due to its time demand, it would be necessary in order to confirm the entire applicability of the results. An advantage with the framework and the monitoring environment, however, is that they allow tailored use and only partial application of the selected parts of the dependability framework and monitoring environment, respectively.

1.4 Method

A literature study has been conducted in order to get a picture of the current achievements and needs and thus formulate clear objectives. A dependability framework has been derived and alternative ways of defining, controlling and achieving dependability throughout the system life-cycle, are presented.

Secondly, an integrity approach has been carried out, including deduction of a general integrity definition on a system and component level in the relation to risk and dependability notions. Further, a risk analysis framework has been deduced and a testing approach conducted, covering real-time, dependability and integrity testing aspects.

The issues related to real-time requirements and distribution were examined and discussed, among these performance, effectiveness, and real-time databases.

Guidelines on testing have been proposed. This has been followed by a detailed approach to active monitoring as a means of dependability enhancement, which integrates the results from the previous chapters and gives guidelines to their collected utilization. An architecture for monitoring environment was designed and the main issues discussed. The developed monitoring environment architecture measures the degree of requirements fulfillment, relates it to the pre-defined, measurable system-level expectations and dynamically adapts the system in real time, based on quality metrics, risk analysis, cost evaluation, control theory, neural networks, data acquisition and system knowledge management, thus integrating the previously obtained results regarding these issues.

Finally, interviews with experts and system developers were conducted to obtain feedback on the results and verify usefulness of the ideas.

1.5 Outline of the thesis

Chapter two gives an introduction into the dependability based former achievements and derives a dependability framework defining dependability in terms of attributes and criteria, and suggesting ways of quantifying those. Further, proposition for means and process of dependability achievement is made.

Chapter three concentrates on system integrity, treating it as one of the non-functional sub-domains of dependability. The concept of integrity is defined and related to integrity level and risk containment. A new approach to risk and vulnerability handling, being closely linked to integrity, is deduced. This will serve as a basis for knowledge management in the monitoring environment presented in chapter 6.

Real-time issues with emphasis on requirements under the different life-cycle stages, performance and concurrency control, are discussed in chapter four.

Chapter five treats the issues of distributes systems, particularly main characteristics, requirements and active distributed databases.

A monitoring framework for distributed real-time systems has been developed and architecture for a monitoring environment designed. In addition, guidelines for design of a monitoring environment have been proposed and presented in chapter 6. Among the issues related to monitoring that have been treated directly or recalled from the preceding chapters are the ones of distribution, real-time, control theory, correctness, testing[2], programming languages, cost-efficiency, dependability requirements, active databases, maintenance and integrity. As such, the monitoring approach integrates the overall parts of the study and ends up with a proposal for architecture of a monitoring environment as well as general guidelines.

The study concludes with a presentation of feedback obtained from discussions and interviews with system developers and experts from industry and the university. The purpose has been to present the study to the people who have experience from similar issues or who might benefit from the results. Their feedback has been valuable in two ways:
- Verification of usefulness of the study.

---

[2] Including testing of both functional and non-functional requirements. A proposal for the development of a test environment is given, the testing process deduced, and design means for testability discussed.

- Valuable comments on further work, extensions and modifications. Chapter 7 is devoted to presentation of this part.

Conclusions on the results obtained and recommendations for further work are given in chapter 8, followed by bibliography[3].

Appendix A gives a list of definitions of the terminology used along the text.

Due to its unique features well suited for monitoring Erlang has been briefly presented in appendix B. Language characteristics are described, as well as run-time environment characteristics. An introduction into Open Telecom Platform is given and fault tolerance in Erlang discussed.

Appendix C entirely quotes an interview given by an expert from a major international company on basis of the presented results[4].

---

3 Containing both references and useful sources on the relevant topics.
4 Including the dependability framework and the monitoring environment architecture.

Chapter 2: Dependability framework

"Just as we can assert that no product has ever been created in a single moment of inspiration ... nobody has ever produced a set of requirements for any product in a similarly miraculous manner. These requirements may well begin with an inspirational moment but, almost certainly, the emergent bright idea will be developed by iterative processes of evaluation until it is thought to be worth starting to pull pencil to paper. Especially when the product is entirely new, the development of a set of requirements may well depend upon testing initial ideas in some depth."
W.H. Mayall, *Principles in Design*, 1979

2.1 Introduction

Regardless of its nature, judgment of every system's success is based on a trade off between a number of factors, including time to develop, reliability, maintainability, costs, timing characteristics, etc. One can distinguish between system costs and development process on the one side, and system characteristics on the other. The system characteristics are further grouped into functional and non-functional requirements. As will be shown, the notion of dependability covers both functional and non-functional system requirements.

Being able to derive, communicate and measure both functional and non-functional requirements in early stages of a systems life-cycle is a crucial issue in almost all projects involving the development of computing systems. In telecommunication systems, for instance, dependability demands on a system are the main factor influencing the business model's ability to remain competitive in an open market.

Too often the unstated but essential non-functional system requirements go unsatisfied, making the system unacceptable. One wishes therefore to be able to specify, implement, measure and monitor the system dependability requirements at all stages of a system life-cycle. Such a process will demand integration of software engineering in the overall management activities (recall TQM[5]) with respect to processes, products and personnel at all company levels and in accordance with the policy statement. As data are collected across projects within an organization, the process and measurements can also be used as the basis for risk assessment and cost estimation. The dependability factors support the identification of risk areas. The measurements provide the mechanism for monitoring progress toward migrating those risks.

2.2 History and the current achievements

Some contributions have already been made in attempts to make a general definition of system dependability. The concept of quality factors originated in the late 1970s in conjunction with the research and development of software development technology. The factors provide the definitions of quality required of a software product. The software measurements, or "metrics", provide the technology by which the factors could be measured. Early work was done by Boehm [Boehm 1981], McCall [McCall 1977], Bowen [Bowen, 1985], Maurine and others. These efforts had much in common, identifying sets of factors or characteristics, related attributes, criteria, and metrics. Boehm took a utility view in identifying seven characteristics of quality while McCall and co-workers took a life-cycle view in identifying 11 factors of quality. The McCall work also had extended the concept of metrics from measurements of code characteristics to also include measurements early in the development phases and in later phases. Further development by Bowen, Maurine and others (Grady, Deutch, Evans, Arthur) have refined the factors or added additional factors to consider. Table 1 [Marciniak, 1994] compares the factors identified by some efforts.

---

5 "Total Quality Management."

McCall, 1977	Boehm, 1978	Bowen, 1985	Maurine, 1983	Others[6]
Correctness		Correctness	Correctness	Correctness
Reliability	Reliability	Reliability	Reliability	Reliability
Efficiency	Efficiency	Efficiency	Efficiency	Efficiency
Usability	Human Engineering	Usability	Usability	Usability
Integrity		Integrity	Integrity	Integrity
Maintainability	Understandability	Maintainability	Maintainability	Maintainability
Flexibility	Modifiability	Flexibility	Flexibility	Flexibility
Testability	Testability	Verifiability	Testability	Testability
Portability	Portability	Portability	Portability	Portability
Reusability		Reusability	Reusability	Reusability
Interoperability		Interoperability	Interoperability	Interoperability
		Survivability		Survivability
			Intraoperability	
		Expandability		Manageability
				Functionality
				Supportability

Table 1: Earlier contributions on quality factors

In each case, the factors are given formal definitions. McCall relates each one of the factors to a given stage in project life-cycle, while Bowen refines this concept further by organizing the factors by:
- *Product performance*: how well does the software function in its normal environment?
- *Product design*: how valid (appropriate) is the design with respect to requirements, verification and maintenance?
- *Product adaption*: how easy is it to adapt the software for use beyond its original intended use?

McCall defines each of the factors and adds ratings for quantification to each of them. Moreover, the quality factors are management oriented and in order to introduce a dimension of quantification, the management orientation is translated into a software related viewpoint by defining a set of criteria for each factor. For each set of factors, related criteria and

---

6 Grady and Caswell (1987); Deutsch and Willlis (1988); Evans and Marciniak (1985); Arthur (1985)

metrics are identified. The metrics are measurements of whether the attributes exist or not and to what degree.

The key contribution of the work done in software quality factors in relation to software engineering is the established framework. The framework facilitates quality goals (factors) of a software product to be identified, relates the goals to the software product in terms of attributes and criteria for their existence and then provides measurements to assure they are being built into the software product as it evolves. This goal-oriented approach provides a quality focused control system to the development effort, augmenting the traditional quality assurance practices. The two significant references on software measurement frameworks take a goal/question/metric paradigm [Basili, 1992] and an experimentation perspective [Basili and co-workers, 1986].

Further, a number of international standards have been developed to help better focus on crucial dependability requirements that add value to designing integrity in products to achieve the desired dependability. The IEC 300 series of International Standards provides proper guidance for dependability specifications and sets criteria for product performance evaluation. Dependability standards complement the existing ISO 9001 series of Quality standards. Among topics of the ISO 9001 standard are:
1. Management responsibility.
2. Quality system.
3. Contract review.
4. Design control.
5. Document control.
6. Purchasing.
7. Purchaser supplied control.
8. Product identification and traceability.
9. Process control.
10. Inspection and testing.
11. Inspection, measuring and test equipment.
12. Inspection and test status.
13. Control and non-conforming products.
14. Corrective action.
15. Handling, storage, packing and delivery.
16. Quality records.

17. Internal quality audits.
18. Training.
19. Servicing.
20. Statistical techniques.

Software maturity levels are related to the different standards. One can expect that ISO 9001 certified software producer operates at the maturity level called managed.

At the managed level of maturity, not only is a successful way to develop software defined, but, in addition, the software process is monitored quantitatively. In particular, meeting these high quality goals is assessed through quantitative measurements.

2.3 On the impairments to dependability

For the purpose of the forthcoming formulations, some terminology for the different stages of situations where something has gone wrong needs to be introduced. The creation and manifestation mechanisms of faults, errors and failures can be summarized as follows:

A system *failure* occurs when the delivered service deviates from fulfilling the system function, the latter being what the system is aimed at. An *error* is that part of the system state which is liable to lead to subsequent failure: an error affecting the service is an indication that a failure occurs or has occurred. The adjudged or hypothesized cause of an error is a *fault* [Randell 1998]. Hence, the following relationship can be induced:
Fault -> error -> failure -> fault ... The point where one has to start can be seen as the one where action can be taken to make a difference.

[Siewiorek 1992] presents three fault notions which can lead to an error: *permanent, intermittent* and *transient* fault. A permanent fault can be induced by physical defect or incorrect design. Causes of an intermittent fault can be incorrect design or unstable hardware, while unstable environment will cause a transient fault. Further, incorrect design or operator mistake can directly lead to an error (state).

A fault is active when it produces an error. An active fault is either an internal fault previously dormant and activated by the computation process or an external fault. Most internal faults cycle between their dormant and active states. Physical faults can directly affect the hardware components only, whereas human-made faults can affect any component.

An error may be latent or detected. An error is latent when it has not been recognized as such. An error is detected by a detection algorithm or mechanism. An error may disappear before being detected. An error may, and in general does, propagate: by propagating, an error creates other - new- error(s). The new errors may be latent or detected independently of the kind of error that generated them. During operation, the presence of active faults is determined only by the detection of errors.

A failure occurs when an error passes through the system-user interface and affects the service delivered by the system. A component failure results in a fault (1) for the system which contains the component and (2) as viewed by the other component(s) with which it interfaces; the failure modes of the failed component then become fault types for the components interacting with it.

For example, the result of a programmer's error is a dormant fault in the written software; upon activation the fault becomes active and produces an error; if and when the erroneous data affect the delivered service, a failure occurs.

As an extreme, any fault can be viewed as a permanent design fault. Indeed, most of the effort should be put under the design phase.

A system may not, and generally does not, always fail in the same way. The ways a system can fail are its failure modes. These can be characterized according to the three different viewpoints:
1. Domain. Failures can be connected to:
   - timing
   - value.
2. Perception by several users, there are two kinds:
   - consistent

- inconsistent (byzantine).
3. Consequences on environment, at least two kinds:
   - benign
   - catastrophic.

2.4 Software aspects of dependability

Software engineering literature offers extensible resources on the topics such as various software life-cycle models, development methods and processes, cost evaluation and quality assurance. Each one of these plays a determining part in the dependability achievement process and undoubtedly deserves closer consideration. Certain aspects can, in the context of this study, be enhanced and given some general improvement guidelines, having dependability achievement as an objective. However due to time limitations, these aspects are only being touched upon rather shortly and referred to in the existing resources [Somerville 1997], [Pressman 2001] and [Kan 1995][7].

Software forms a part of a product or a system to provide specific application and can not function by itself. The software aspects of dependability address the software components within the system in the context of dependability attribute related requirements.

Software is characterized by its application function, operating environment, size, complexity, process priority handling, memory management, parameters, installation and upgrade processes.

The life-cycle of software is very much intertwined with the life-cycle of its parent system. Figure 2.1 is attempted to relate the software life-cycle phases with the conventional product life-cycle phases.

---

[7] Also a comprehensive reading in software development process models, quality metrics, statistical methods, Total Quality Management and standards.

Design Guidelines for a Monitoring Environment Concerning Distributed Real-Time Systems

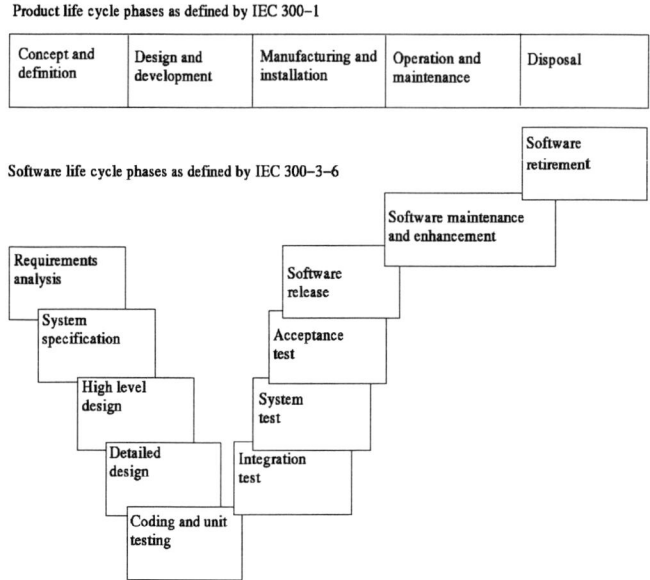

Figure 2.1: Relationship between product life-cycle phases and software life-cycle phases

The figure gives an overview of the most common stages of the two development processes and their mutual timing aspects. In case of the most well known, waterfall model, it has been found that 40% of time is spent on preparation, 20% on actual programming, while testing and error correction take another 40%. More recent figures show a 60-15-25 distribution of successful projects. The larger amount of time spent on the analysis and design is justified by the observation that it is far better to prevent errors than to try to repair the effects of these errors during testing. Early introduced errors are extremely expensive.

It is referred to the related software engineering literature for a more detailed consideration of each of the phases. Note that terminology varies considerably among the different presentations on the topic (e.g. overall design vs. high level design, enhancement vs. revision). Whenever possible and convenient, this document will tend to use the already established and most descriptive terms.

2.5 Towards a general definition of dependability

One can argue for a number of different definitions of dependability. Most of the formulations proposed so far have attempted to include a set of general quality characteristics which would cover a required level of trust in the system. Generally, dependability can be considered as "that property of a computer system such that reliance can justifiably be placed on the service it delivers" [Barbacci 1995]. Formulation of a system's dependability and the related attributes should in each case include a selection of the most critical attributes, based on the system's nature and requirements, at the same time taking a group of critical aspects into account:
- The stakeholders' requirements.
- Budget of the project.
- The expected evolution of the system.
- The operational environment.
- Interaction with other systems.
- Safety requirements.
- Security requirements.
- Criticality of the correctness and timing aspects.
- Availability needs.
- Development methods, etc.

Dependability embraces a broad spectrum of management and engineering disciplines to guide product integrity through its life-cycle process to ensure the required quality. Dependability enhances the abilities of product performance through analysis, measures and control of its life-cycle stage characteristics. Integrity is, on the other hand, concerned (based on the formulations proposed later in this document) with design characteristics.

[Howden, Huang 1994] presents software trustability as a measure of dependability, which again is based on detectability. The detectability of a method is the conditional probability that it will detect faults. The model proposed provides a framework for a software evaluation approach that can incorporate different aspects of dependability measurement and use different evaluation techniques from different stages of development.

2.5.1 Framework deduction

The definition proposed is motivated by the earlier contributions of McCall[8], while the approach, framework, definitions and metrics contain significant differences. The reader is therefore advised to refer to the dependability definition deduced in this text when interpreting the results and analysis presented in this document.

The notion of *dependability* will within the context of this document and for the purpose of later references, be treated as **the level of trustworthiness of a computing system. As such, dependability allows a predefined degree of reliance to be justifiably placed on the service the system delivers.** De facto definition of software dependability will however always consist of two levels: intrinsic product quality and customer satisfaction. As the latter one is subjective and based on expectations, its fraction is unknown.

[Tseng, Fogg 1999] in their article on credibility of computing systems argue when trustworthiness matters in computing systems:
- When computers act as knowledge repositories.
- When computers instruct or tutor users.
- When computers report measurements.
- When computers report on work performed.
- When computers report on their own state.
- When computers run simulations.
- When computers help render virtual environments.

The structure of the framework is as illustrated on figure 2.2.

---

8 [McCall 1977].

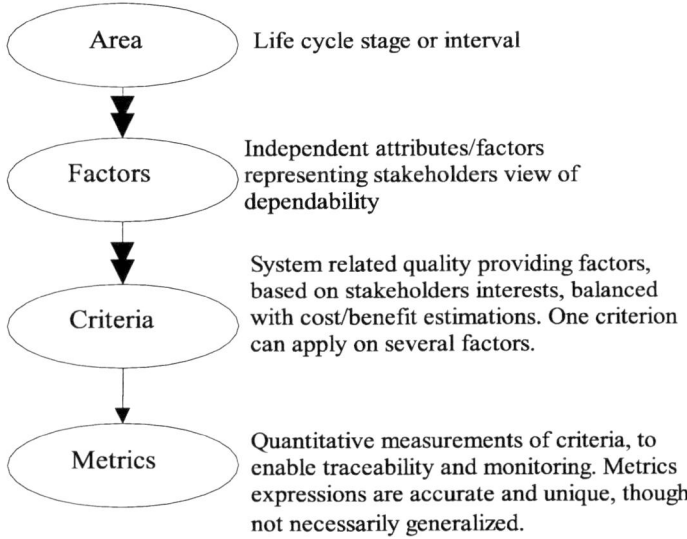

Figure 2.2: Software dependability framework[9]

At the highest level of the framework are the project life-cycle stages which, for the purpose of the definition, are grouped into three categories: operations, revision and transition.

The level below life-cycle stage categories contains a listing of dependability factors. The factors comprise a definition of dependability and represent attributes or characteristics of the software that a user, customer or producer would relate to its overall level of trustworthiness. Note that the definition assumes mutual orthogonality[10] of the factors. The dependability factors provide:
- A goal-oriented methodology for measuring system dependability.
- Another dimension by which system requirements can be addressed complementing the traditional, functional, schedule and budgetary requirements, typically specified for computing systems.
- A life-cycle perspective to software, i.e., identifying attributes important in a software product that will have impact later in its life-cycle.
- A basis for process improvement (TQM).

---

9 The double arrows indicate one-to-many-relationship.
10 Orthogonality in this sense also implies independence.

The third level of the framework provides the criteria or system properties that relate to the factors and their existence provides the related characteristics of dependability.

The fourth level provides the metrics or measurements that evaluate the degree to which the criteria exist. These are quantitative measures derivable from any attribute or software life-cycle and as such allow monitoring and traceability of dependability factors as defined in the requirements specification. The expression defining each metric is unique although not necessarily generalizable to several systems. Software metrics can be defined as:

The continuous application of measurement-based techniques to the software development process and the products to supply meaningful and timely management information, together with the use of those techniques to improve that process and its products.

Apart from the mathematical expression, a metric should be represented by its:
- Costs.
- Benefits.
- Impact: an indication of whether the metric may be used to alter or halt the project.
- Target value: numerical value of the metric that is to be achieved to meet dependability requirements.
- Factors related to the metric.
- Tools: software or hardware tools that are used to gather and store data, compute the metric, and analyze the results.
- Application: a description of how the metric is used and its area of application.
- Data items necessary for computing the metric.
- Interpretation of the results of the metric computation.
- Considerations: metric assumptions and appropriateness.

Figure 2.3 gives an overview of the entire framework. At each level a formal definition of the describing elements is derived.

2.5.1.1 Life-cycle stage categories

The dependability defining factors in the framework are related to the three categories of life-cycle stages:
- Operations: the stage when the system is being utilized and offering the services in accordance with the requirements specification.
- Revision: the stage when system control and changes are being undertaken.
- Transition: adaption of the system for use beyond its originally intended use.

For the purpose of a consistent definition, the three categories are distinguished, although, depending on the nature of the system under consideration, they may interact or appear in an unpredictable order.

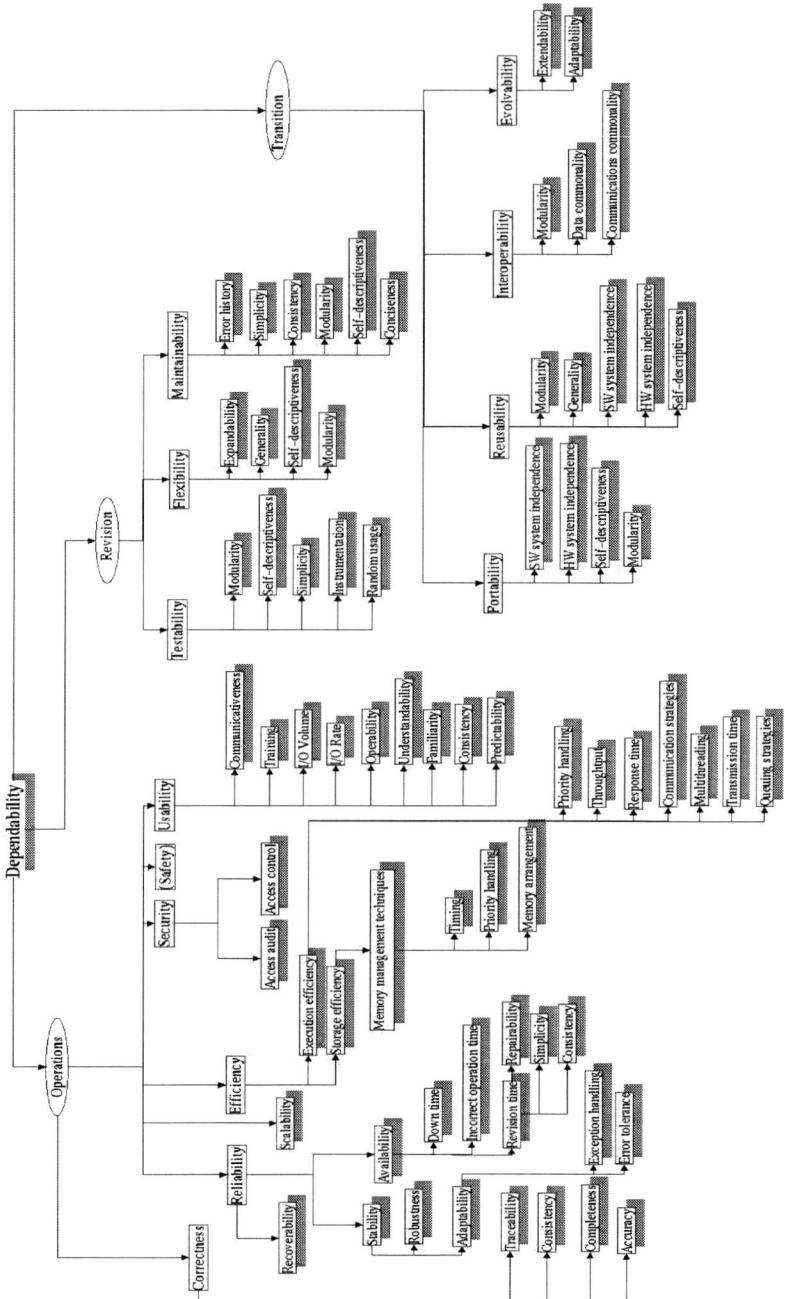

Figure 2.3: Dependability framework definition

The purpose and the intended length of use of the system will influence the level of priority/importance of the life-cycle-stage categories and the related dependability factors. A customer or a user, for example, of a newly developed system is initially concerned, from a dependability viewpoint, with how well the product operates. For example, does it perform the functions desired correctly, reliably, as efficiently as required, so that the user can operate it well and securely?

If the system is going to be used for any length of time, then the concern becomes whether it is easy to maintain, change and test to see if the fixes and changes have been made correctly. Longer life-cycle implications include how easy the product is to port to another environment or a new version of an operating system or a new hardware suite, how easy will it be to reuse when a new generation of the systems is built, and how easy it is to interface with other systems?

This dependability focus relates to the process of developing and supporting the software during its life-cycle and the effort required during this process.

2.5.1.2 Deduction of system dependability factors

Each of the dependability factors[11] (recall level two of the framework on figure 2.3) is related to one (and only one) of the life-cycle stage categories and clearly defined. A rating expression is further added to each factor. This approach opens for a communication of system dependability and quantifies the dependability factors to allow traceability, quality assessment and system improvement.

The ratings, however, are only examples of quantitative dependability goals that can be established using the dependability measurement framework. Below is each of the factors defined.

Correctness: The degree to which a system satisfies its specifications and fulfills the software standards and users' mission objectives.

---

11 Also called attributes.

Rating expression:

$$Correctness = 1 - \frac{\sum_{n=1}^{N}(Weight * RepDistinctDeviations_n)}{\sum_{i=1}^{I}(OpTimeUnits_i * (OrigSystSize + ExtensionSize)_i)} \quad [Eq.2.1]$$

The above expression is the rating of correctness factor, where:
- *Weight:* the deviations can be weighted by defining a number of criticality levels and assigning a level to each reported distinct deviation.
- *OpTimeUnits*: number of operating hours, i.e., actively functioning hours of the system.
- *OrigSystSize*: the original size of the system related to the number of actively operating hours. This number will in most of the cases equal one.
- *ExtensionSize*: the extension of the system relative to the original size.
- *RepDistinctDeviations*: number of reported deviations. Note that the deviations are normally reported by the users and that each type of deviation is registered only once for the related system size. The kinds of deviations indicating incorrectness of the system are, for example:
  - Inaccuracies.
  - Deviations from standards.
  - Redundant or not desirable values/behaviour.
  - Missing or inconsistent service(parts), regardless of whether specified in requirements or not. The written requirements should be fulfilled as specified, while a shortage of the non-specified ones is considered as incorrectness too.

The total system size is a sum of OrigSystSize and ExtensionSize. Both OrigSystSize and ExtensionSize are measured in the same manner and can be based on the service extension, number of lines (NOL), working hours, data volume, etc. For each total system size, the number of actively operating time units is recorded, and the sum of their product (denominator) is related to the number of reported distinct deviations, each deviation multiplied by the belonging pre-defined level of weight. For each system size, the value under the sum sign in front of the fraction is calculated. Finally, the sum of all the values belonging to the fraction part of the expression is subtracted from one to get a quality representing value of the factor.

The *OpTimeUnits* variable is to be defined in a manner which ensures a large value of denominator compared to the numerator, resulting in a sum of fraction values which is smaller than one. Note that this time variable is measured relative to the actual operating time, i.e., the time the system is active in contrast to only being available. The definition of an active system can be based on the use of any combination of the system resources, or only a particular one (e.g. the processor). The final expression value gives a rating for the correctness of the system.

Reliability:
1. Extent to which a system will perform without any failures within a specified period of time. [Bowen 1985]
2. The probability of failure-free software operation for a specified period of time in a specified environment. [Lyu 1995]

We are interested in the time, T, it takes before a system or a component fails after first having been put into use.

Rating:

$$Reliability\ R(t) = 1 - \sum_{t=0}^{T} \sum_{n=0}^{N} \frac{(DistinctFailure * Weight * WorkLoad)_n}{OpTimeUnits_t * (OrigSystSize + ExtensionSize)_t} [Eq. 2.2]$$

where:
- n is index of failure.
- t is the index of the operational time unit related to the size of the system.
- DistinctFailure is the the number of distinct failures corresponding to the weight and workload of the system.
- Weight is the pre-defined level of criticality of the failure.
- WorkLoad is proportional to the intensity of resource use. The definition can be based on any resource: data flow, memory usage, processor, number of simultaneous users, etc.
- OpTimeUnits is as above defined as the number of operating hours, i.e., actively functioning hours of the system.
- OrigSystSize and ExtensionSize represent the current amount of service offered by the system at time t.

When subtracted from one, the expression under the sum signs gives a rating for system reliability, which is a value less than or equal to one. The value of the expression under the sum signs is always expected to be between 0 and 1, inclusive. This requires the parameters within the expression[12] to be defined in a way which clearly represents the changes in system reliability, at the same time guaranteeing the final value to be within the given range[13].

Note that all the parameters are considered to be discrete variables, and the time intervals can be system specific. Assuming that the unit of measure of workload is a product of time unit[14] and the system or resource size, the final expression is dimensionless. To deduce the acceptance margins of reliability, experiments can be undertaken by monitoring the system and varying one parameter at time.

Reliability is for the purpose of our definition divided up into the main sub-factors:
- *Recoverability*: the ability of the system to restore a resource to a state[15] in which it can perform the required actions.

Rating:

$$Recoverability = \frac{1}{N} * \sum_{n=0}^{N} \frac{NoRestorations}{NoFailures} \quad [Eq. 2.3]$$

where:
- N is the number of time units.
- NoRestorations denotes the number of restorations.
- NoFailures denotes the number of failures.

A more complex expression will be likely to include parameters such as:
- System size (complexity and service extension).
- Workload.

---

12 Value of all parameters except DistinctFailure will be based on the their definitions.
13 That is, between 0 and 1, inclusive.
14 The time-part of the definition of workload is based on only active time period(s) of the system/component/resource operation, which are summed up and multiplied by the system/component/resource size to obtain workload value.
15 State: the values assumed at a given instant by the variables that define the specified or expected characteristics of the system.

- Failure weight.
- Only distinct failures.
- Sequential faults.
- Origins of failures (related to the development stage).
- Fault prevention and tolerance mechanisms (size and cost of).

• *Stability*: the ability of the system to preserve the specified or expected state for a given period of time, without performing unexpected actions.

Rating:

$$Stability = 1 - \sum_{n=0}^{N} \frac{NumberOfUnexpectedStateChanges}{OpTimeUnits * (OrigSystSise + ExtensionSize)_n} \quad [Eq.2.4]$$

where:
- NumberOfUnexpectedStateChanges is the number of state changes of the system deviating from the expectations.
- OpTimeUnits is defined as the number of operating hours, i.e., actively functioning hours of the system, as defined previously.
- OrigSystSize and ExtensionSize represent the current amount of service offered by the system at time t.
- n is number of the current time unit.

• *Availability*: the degree to which a system or component is operational and accessible when required for use [Glos 1993]. More often expressed as the probability that the software will be functioning in a satisfactory manner at a given future time, conditional upon its satisfactory functioning at a defined start time [Rook 1990].

Rating:

$$Availability = 1 - (Avg\ fraction\ of\ down\ time) = 1 - \frac{1}{N} \sum_{n=0}^{N} \frac{MTTD_n + MTTR_n}{MTBF_n} \quad [Eq.2.5]$$

where:
- MTTD is the mean time to detect.
- MTTR is the mean time to repair.
- MTBF is the mean time between failures.
- n is the sequential number of the current failure.

Figure 2.4 below illustrates the relationship between the parameters used to define availability. In non-functional terms, availability can simply be defined as the length of uptime per a time unit (e.g. year). The system is available between restart and an error occurrence. One example is

$$Availability = \frac{\sum_{i=1}^{I}(Uptime\ in\ period\ i)}{\sum_{i=1}^{I}(Total\ expected\ in\ service\ time\ for\ period\ i)} \quad [Eq.2.6]$$

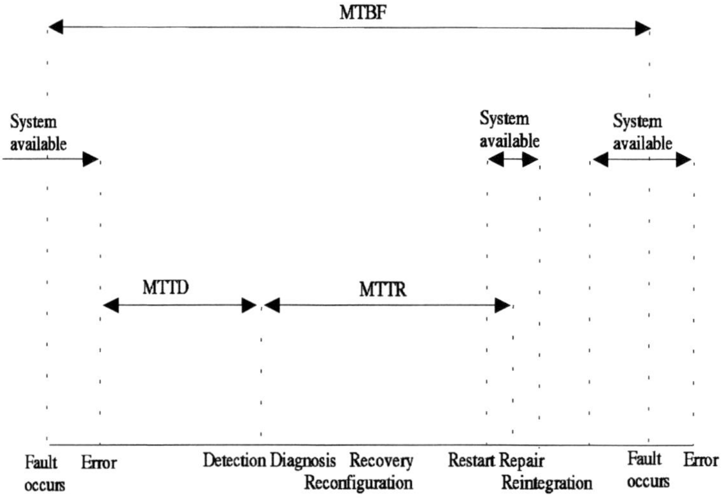

Figure 2.4: Terminology of availability [Siewiorek 1992]

Scalability: the ability of the system to support rapid and extensive variations in the number of users without requiring any changes.

Rating:

$$Scalability:\ the\ number\ of\ simultaneous\ users\ supported\ by\ the\ system\ (without\ decrease\ in\ the\ quality\ of\ service\ level)\ before\ any\ changes\ need\ to\ be\ made. \quad [Eq.2.7]$$

scalability definition in this sense will depend on a number of factors:
- System size (service extent and complexity).

- Workload.
- Expected variations in user numbers.
- Extent of supported collaboration for group-based services.

Efficiency: (Considered as a synonym to performance.) The degree to which a system or component performs its designated functions with minimum consumption of resources.

The definition can refer to various situations. One tends towards a maximum utilization of resources (e.g. storage space, processing time, communication time). The factor is in this sense equalized with the systems performance, i.e. the quality of service measured as a function of available resources and inputs.

Rating:

$$Efficiency = 1 - \frac{Actual\ resource\ utilization}{Allocated\ resource\ utilization} \quad [Eq.\ 2.8]$$

In case of most systems, performance refers to the response time or throughput as seen by the users. For real-time or reactive systems it is the time required to respond to events, most often based on the exploitation of the overall system resources. Real-time systems must meet performance and predictability requirements to be correct. Other systems have less stringent requirements, but responsiveness limits the amount of work processed, so it limits the systems effectiveness and the productivity of its users.

Safety: The extent to which the system fulfills the environmental and health-related requirements and standards concerning human factors. Safety can also be seen in connection with the system code and infrastructure protectiveness by questioning how easily it can be harmed or misused.

Although no doubt extremely important, this factor will not be further examined during the course of this work. The general definition of dependability is expected to contain this factor, as for systems where safety is one of the issues this will be one of the most influencing factors of dependability.

Security: extent to which the software will perform without failures due to unauthorized access to the code (including sabotage) or data within a specified time period [Bowen 1985]. The notion of security concentrates on application and service trustworthiness.

A link between security and correctness (often called integrity) is the ability to prevent misuse or unauthorized access of systems functionalities or contents, a definition which in most cases makes it synonymous to confidentiality ("the nonoccurrence of unauthorized disclosure of information" [Lyu 1995]).

Rating:

$$Security = 1 - \frac{\frac{1}{NLevels}\sum_{l=1}^{NLevels} Level_l \frac{1}{TB_l} \sum_{i=1}^{TB}(TTBSL_{il})}{\sum_{n=1}^{NSize}(OpTimeUnits_n *(OrigSystSize+ExtensionSize)_n)} \quad [Eq.2.9]$$

where:
- NLevels is a predefined number of levels of security breaches.
- Level is the numerical weight description of the breach level.
- TB is the number of times a certain security level is breached (read "times breached").
- TTBSL is the number of times a certain security level is breached (read "time to breach security level").
- OpTimeUnits is as above defined as the number of operating hours, i.e., actively functioning hours of the system.
- OrigSystSize and ExtensionSize represent the current amount of service offered by the system at time t.
- n is number of the current time unit.
- Nsize is the number of times the system has changed the size.

The definition of system size is application specific and can be based on complexity, service extent, etc. The expression above gives a probability function for the system security over a given period of operational time of the system. A number of security breach levels (categories) are predefined and assigned a numerical value. Each time a security barrier is breached, its level and time to breach are detected.

In the numerator, an average of TTBSL is taken for each security level (remember that one or more security levels can be breached by several users simultaneously). This value is multiplied by the level weight and the calculation is repeated for each level. The numerator is divided by the number of levels. Changes in system size are taken into account by multiplying the number of time units of systems operation by the size of the system related to it. Note that OpTimeUnits and TTBSL - parameters have the same unit of measure. The rating is not cumulative, that is level 3 breach does not count as level 1, level 2 and level 3 breach with additive weightings, although weighting values should correspond to the levels.

Usability: The ease with which a user can learn to operate, prepare inputs, and interpret outputs of a system or component. [IEEE 1985]

The notion of usability concentrates on the relative effort needed to learn, operate, prepare input and interpret output of a system.

Rating:

$$Usability = 1 - \frac{1}{NUsers} \sum_{l=1}^{NUsers} \frac{TTL_l * LevelWeight_l}{\sum_{n=1}^{NSize} (OpTimeUnits_n * (OrigSystSize + ExtensionSize)_n)} \quad [Eq.2.10]$$

where:
- TTL: "Time to Learn" is the time the user has spent towards achieving a pre-defined level of knowledge (has the same unit of measure as OpTimeUnits).
- LevelWeight: the pre-defined level of knowledge a user can achieve.
- OpTimeUnits: the time the system (related to a size) has been functioning actively (i.e. at least one of the system resources has been occupied at a time).
- OrigSystSize and ExtensionSize represent the current amount of service offered by the system at each time.

The expression is based on the effort a user makes to become acquainted with the system to a certain level, depending on the system complexity. A number of important constraints to this rating are:

- User satisfaction.
- Ease of preparing inputs and interpreting outputs.
- Predictability.
- Familiarity with the system.

The attribute criteria presented in the section to follow and illustrated by figure 2.3 represent the most important factors. A number of such factors are descriptive and as such impossible to include into the rating expression.

Testability: the degree to which a system or component facilitates the establishment of test criteria and the performance of tests to determine whether those criteria have been met [Glos 1993]. More often expressed as the probability that the program will fail under test if it contains at least one fault.

The factor is related to the effort required to test a program to ensure if it performs its intended function.

Rating:

$$Testability = \frac{(Number\ of\ Faults\ Detectable\ Under\ Testing)}{(Total\ Number\ of\ Potential\ Faults)} \quad [Eq.2.11]$$

The term "test coverage" is frequently used to communicate testability of a system. Test coverage is the degree of representativeness of the test results to the actual system state.

Some of the influencing constraints are
- Independence of the test environment from the overall system environment.
- Unbiased test implementation and use of random, representative input.
- Recognition of sequential faults.

When a dependability assessment has to be derived from the observation of a series of failure-free test executions (a common need for software subject to "ultra - high reliability" requirements), measures of testability can, in theory, be used to draw inferences on program correctness (and hence its probability of failure under operation).

Flexibility: The level of effort with which a system or a component can be modified for use in applications or environments other than those for which it is specifically designed. [IEEE 1985]

Rating:

$$Flexibility = 1 - \frac{1}{N} \sum_{n=1}^{N} \frac{(Cost\, of\, Modification)_n}{(Expected\, Benefit\, Increase)} \quad [Eq.2.12]$$

where
- N: number of modifications conducted.

The definitions of cost and benefit in the expression above can be based on time, service extent, time, money or the similar. It is however assumed that the unit of measure is the same in both numerator and denominator.

Among issues that should be addressed when planning for flexibility are:
- Market growth or decrease.
- New stakeholders.
- New technologies.
- New service concepts.
- Regulations.
- Environment changes.

Maintainability: The level of effort with which a system or a component can be modified to correct faults, improve performance or other factors or adapt to a changed environment within a specified time period.

Rating:

$$Maintainability = 1 - \frac{(Modification\, effort)}{(Initial\, Development\, Effort)} \quad [Eq.2.13]$$

This is a user oriented definition. One can also define the rating as a ratio between effort to change and degree of change or adjustment made to the system; a definition which protects interests of both product developer/service provider and the user.

Some systems will have special maintainability requirements, such as:
- Correction time limits.
- System availability during maintenance.
- Cost/budget constraints.
- Safety requirements.
- Only certain types of maintenance accepted (e.g. no corrective maintenance).

These and other constraints are to be taken into consideration in addition to the rating parameters included in the expression. The non-compulsory factors of all attributes can be assigned a weight or a degree of importance and used to formulate an optimization problem for management of maintenance or any other attribute.

Portability: The relative effort required to transport a system or component, originally developed on one computer or operating system, to another environment.

Rating:

$$Portability = 1 - \frac{(Effort\ to\ Port\ a\ System)}{(Effort\ to\ Develop\ the\ System)} \quad [Eq.2.14]$$

A number of non-quantitative parameters and constraints will apply, depending on the system requirements and nature. Examples include:
- Degree of component independence.
- National and international standards.

Reusability: Relative effort needed to convert a system or component for use in another application. [Bowen 1985]

$$Reusability = 1 - \frac{1}{M} \sum_{i=1}^{M} \frac{(Effort\ to\ convert)_i * (Fraction\ of\ System)_i}{(Effort\ to\ develop\ the\ new\ component)_i} \quad [Eq.2.15]$$

where:
- i: component index.

- M: number of components.

[Sommerville 1997] argues for software reuse as a means for achieving dependability. "Component reuse, of course, does not just mean the reuse of code. It is possible to reuse specifications and designs." [Sommerville 1997] further argues that costs, software development time and process risk are reduced, human resources are used more effectively and organizational standards can easily be embodied in reusable components.

Interoperability: relative effort to couple the software of one system to the software of another system. [Bowen 1985]

This factor further concerns the ability of the two systems to exchange, use and interpret the exchanged information.

Rating:

$$Interoperability = 1 - \frac{(Effort\,to\,Couple)}{(Effort\,to\,Develop)} \quad [Eq.2.16]$$

Evolvability: relative effort needed to make architectural system changes such that the result can be extended service, additional properties or increased number of users.

Rating:

$$Evolvability = 1 - \frac{(Cost\,of\,Extension)}{(Value\,of\,Extended\,Service)} \quad [Eq.2.17]$$

Note that parameters in numerator and denominator have the same units of measure, which can be based on value, amount of work, size of the system or the similar.

Each of the attributes may have a different meaning, as well as different degree of priority for the selected groups of stakeholders.

As indicated above, the dependability related attributes may be emphasized to a greater or lesser extent depending on the application intended for the computer system concerned. Further, reaching a certain dependability level and at the same time finding the most cost-effective way to achieve it, as well as mastering the need for evolution and adjustment of the system, can be treated as a control and optimization problem.

In their article, [Fraser, Vaishnavi 1997] present a formal specification maturity model (FSM) defining five system maturity levels:
1. Initial.
   - Cannot be repeated without the same personnel.
   - Capability and specifications are a characteristic of individuals, not organizations.
2. Repeatable.
   - A stable progress has been achieved.
   - New applications planned and managed based on experience with similar projects.
3. Defined.
   - A process is defined as a basis for consistent implementation and better understanding.
   - Risk of reducing advanced solutions is greatly reduced.
   - Process includes readiness criteria, inputs, standards and procedures, verification, outputs and completion criteria.
4. Managed.
   - Organization-initiated comprehensive process measurement and analysis.
   - Predictable trends in process and product quality.
   - Quantitative, computerized and experience based management.
5. Optimizing.
   - A foundation for continuously improving and optimizing the process.
   - The best software engineering practices and innovations are identified and transferred throughout organization.
   - Known types of defects are prevented from recurring.
   - Efforts are made to remove waste results in changing the common causes of inefficiency.

Monitoring within the dependability framework ensures provision of the highest level of system maturity.

2.5.1.3 Deduction of system dependability criteria

The dependability factors from above represent a management-oriented view of software quality. To introduce a dimension of quantification, this management orientation is translated into a system-related viewpoint. This translation is accomplished by defining a set of criteria and metrics for each factor. These criteria define the dependability factors further. Note that one criterion can be related to more than one factor. The criteria are independent characteristics of the system or the system development process by which the dependability can be judged, defined and measured.

These criteria are the basis for recognizing the relationships between the factors as dependability goals for a development effort.

Certain criteria will be system specific and therefore not found in the general dependability definition. Interpretation and meaning of some criteria may, in some cases, differ from the general definition. Also, depending on the system nature, different criteria may have different roles in attribute definition. Examples include:
- A requirement constraint.
- An influencing factor.
- An audit.
- A characteristic.

Below are the definitions of the main attribute-defining criteria deduced.

Dependability attribute: **Correctness**

- Traceability: those characteristics of the software that provide a thread from the requirements to the implementation with respect to the specific development and operational environment.
- Consistency: those characteristics of the software that provide uniform design and implementation techniques and notation.
- Completeness: those characteristics of the software that provide full implementation of the functions required.
- Accuracy: those characteristics of the software that provide the required precision in calculations and outputs.

Dependability attribute: **Reliability**

- Robustness: the degree to which a system or component can function correctly in the presence of invalid inputs or stressful environmental conditions. [Glos 1993]
- Adaptability: those characteristics of the software that make it adjustable to changing environment or unpredicted behaviour.
- Exception handling: treatment of behavioural deviations of the system by categorizing groups of such situations and specifying their treatment.
- Down time: the period of time during which a system or component is not operational or has been taken out of service.
- Incorrect operation time: the period of time during which a system is operational offering incorrect service, regardless of whether a stakeholder is aware of the current state.
- Revision time: the intervals during the system life-cycle at which system control and changes are being undertaken.
- Reparability: the ease with which system changes can be undertaken.
- Simplicity: the degree to which a system or component has a design or implementation that is straightforward and easy to understand.
- Consistency: see the definition of this criterion under correctness attribute.

Dependability attribute: **Efficiency**

- Execution efficiency: those characteristics of the software that provide for minimum processing time.
- Storage efficiency: those characteristics of the software that provide for minimum storage requirements during operation.
- Memory management techniques: the means of achieving optimal memory exploitation.
- Timing: time managing and exploitation.
- Priority handling: the means of optimizing resource exploitation and ensuring correct execution sequence of processes.
- Memory arrangement: division of memory for its optimal usage.
- Throughput: the amount of work that can be performed by a system or a component in a given period of time.
- Response time: the elapsed time between the end of an inquiry or

command to an interactive system and the beginning of the systems response. [Glos 1993]
- Communication strategies: the underlying method used for exchange of data between function and component interfaces.
- Multithreading: the underlying methods used for treatment of several threads simultaneously.
- Transmission time: the amount of time a data package or a signal uses to be transferred between two functions or components.
- Queuing strategies: the underlying methods used to organize sequence of treatment or operation of several elements that share one or more resources and that may be intermittently dependent.

Dependability attribute: **Security**

- Access audit: those characteristics of the software that provide for an audit of the access of software and data. There should be provision for immediate indication of access violation.
- Access control: those characteristics of the software that provide for control of access to software and data.

Dependability attribute: **Usability**

- Communicativeness: those characteristics of the software that provide for ease of input and output assimilation, description and knowledge transformation.
- Training: those characteristics of the software that provide for transition from current operation or initial familiarization.
- I/O volume: the extent of input and output data.
- I/O rate: speed of input and output data flow.
- Operability: those characteristics of the software that determine the procedures concerned with the operation of the software.
- Understandability: the ease with which the systems operation can be comprehended by the user.
- Familiarity: the degree to which the user has previously been involved in use of comparable applications.
- Consistency: see the definition of this criterion under correctness attribute.
- Predictability: the degree to which system behaviour can be foreseen.

Dependability attribute: **Testability**

- Modularity: those characteristics of the software that provide a structure of highly independent components.
- Self-descriptiveness: those characteristics of the software that provide explanation of the system properties.
- Simplicity: see the definition of this criterion under reliability attribute.
- Instrumentation: those characteristics of the software that provide for the measurements of usage or identification of errors.
- Random usage: a varied and unbiased exploitation of the system, as close as possible to a real situation.

Dependability attribute: **Flexibility**

- Expandability: those characteristics of the software that provide for increase of service scope or quality of the system.
- Generality: the degree to which a system or component performs a broad range of functions.
- Self-descriptiveness: see the definition of this criterion under testability attribute.
- Modularity: see the definition of this criterion under testability attribute.

Dependability attribute: **Maintainability**

- Error history: a survey of the previously detected errors.
- Simplicity: see the definition of this criterion under reliability attribute.
- Consistency: see the definition of this criterion under correctness attribute.
- Modularity: see the definition of this criterion under testability attribute.
- Self-descriptiveness: see the definition of this criterion under testability attribute.
- Conciseness: those characteristics of the software that provide for development with minimum amount of contents.

Dependability attribute: **Portability**

- SW system independence: the properties of the software that determine its dependency on the software environment.
- HW system independence: the properties of the software that determine its dependency on the machine environment (hardware).
- Self-descriptiveness: see the definition of this criterion under testability attribute.
- Modularity: see the definition of this criterion under testability attribute.

Dependability attribute: **Reusability**

- Modularity: see the definition of this criterion under testability attribute.
- Generality: see the definition of this criterion under flexibility attribute.
- SW system independence: see the definition of this criterion under portability attribute.
- HW system independence: see the definition of this criterion under portability attribute.
- Self-descriptiveness: see the definition of this criterion under testability attribute.

Dependability attribute: **Interoperability**

- Modularity: see the definition of this criterion under testability attribute.
- Data commonality: those characteristics of the software that provide for use of standard data representations.
- Communications commonality: those characteristics of the software that provide for use of standard protocols and interface routines.

Dependability attribute: **Evolvability**

- Extendibility: see the definition of this criterion under flexibility attribute.

- Adaptability: see the definition of this criterion under reliability attribute.

2.5.1.4 Deduction of criteria related metrics

The criteria related metrics are measurements of whether the criteria exist or not and to what degree. Being evaluative and nonambiguous expressions, metrics are means of employing a cleanroom approach into the system development process. The metrics can be checklists that grade the system software for a particular factor, inspection guidelines that evaluate the software and its documentation for specific factors and information; or quantitative measures of criteria. McCall and Bowen have made significant contributions in defining metrics in [McCall 1977] and [Bowen 1985], respectively. There are three primary reasons to measure level of criteria fulfillment:
1. Determine the current level of system dependability.
2. Predict system dependability level in the future relative to the expected standards.
3. Improve the development process and increase the dependability level.

According to [Pfleeger and Fitzgerald 1991], the collection of metrics associated with a software project can increase development costs by up to 10%. Therefore, the metrics data acquisition should be minimized to the needs of controlling the pre-determined requirement levels. All the overall efforts will result in undesired cost increases beyond the customer requirements, thus reducing the product dependability (which in this sense represents the overall product trustworthiness, consisting of expected product characteristics and cost requirements). Establishment of evaluation expressions in terms of metric probability functions and cost figures allows for treatment of overall system dependability over period of time as an optimization problem.

Software metrics can be classified into three categories: product metrics, process metrics and project metrics. Product metrics are those that describe the characteristics of the product such as size, complexity, design features and performance. Process metrics are those that can be used for software development and maintenance process. Examples include the effectiveness of defect removal during development, pattern of testing defect arrival and the response time of the fixing process. Project metrics are those that describe the project characteristics and execution. Examples include project life-cycle, cost, schedule and productivity.

Software dependability metrics can be considered as a subset of software metrics that focus on the dependability aspects of the product, process and project. Software dependability metrics can further be divided into end-product quality metrics and in-process quality metrics.

The derived metrics should be:
- Simple and computable.
- Empirically and intuitively persuasive.
- Consistent and objective.
- Consistent in its use of units and dimensions.
- Programming language independent.
- An effective mechanism for high quality feedback.
- Tailored to best accommodate the specific system.
- Established before the data collection begins.

The attributes should be controlled during all of the project phases. Metrics are thus needed as a means of measuring the degree of fulfillment. Those measurements required to achieve observability and those required to achieve controllability can be specified. A set of one or more metrics should represent a rating as defined from one or more points of view with a "one-to-one" relationship, meaning that each rating can be assigned a unique value on basis of the corresponding metric values[16].

Thus, ratings are split up into metrics for the purpose of measurability and normalization. Metrics are deduced from the corresponding attribute criteria. One metric can be involved in more than one rating. In most cases metric definitions are system specific and based on detailed system knowledge. General, system independent attribute ratings should be used

---

16 Metrics are considered as detailed, measurable system features whose values directly determine the corresponding value of the rating.

whenever applicable and adjusted to the system under consideration.

According to the definition, each criterion from the section above is to be assigned a metric for its assessment. Dependability metric is a function whose inputs are software data and whose output is a single numerical value that can be interpreted as the degree to which software fulfills a given criterion. The most convenient way of defining a metric is by expressing it by a probability function, having a value between one and zero (where one indicates 100% fulfilled criterion, and zero accordingly) as the outcome. To illustrate the idea, metrics of some exemplar criteria are defined below.

Consistency metric:

$$Consistency = 1 - \frac{Number\ of\ deviations}{Number\ of\ checkpoints} \quad [Eq.2.18]$$

where:
- Deviation: a non-uniform presentation, design, implementation, documentation, data, user interface or behaviour.
- Checkpoint: any system feature, such as:
    -user interface.
    -data I/O.
    -operation.

Examples include procedure consistency and data consistency. Measurement can be based on consistency checklists where a number of consistency levels are classified.

Accuracy metric:

$$Accuracy = \frac{1}{M} \sum_{i=1}^{M} \frac{Required\ Precision\ Level}{Precision\ Level_i} \quad [Eq.2.19]$$

where:
- M: number of measurements.
- Highest precision level has the highest numerical value.
- (Precision Level) >= (Required Precision Level).

Modularity metric:

$$Modularity = 1 - \frac{1}{M} \sum_{i=1}^{M} \frac{NrComp_i}{TotNrComp} \quad [Eq.2.20]$$

where:
- M: number of samples in measurement.
- NrComp: average number of components influenced by error in current function.
- TotNrComp: total number of components/functions in the system, alternatively measured by dependency level or degree of cohesion.
- i: current function index.

Memory arrangement metric:

$$Memory\ arrangement = \frac{PackageSize}{AvailMem} \quad [Eq.2.21]$$

where:
- PackageSize: maximum acceptable size of a new data package.
- AvailMem: total memory available (unoccupied).

Availability metrics:
- Mean Time Between Failures (MTBF).
- Mean Time To Repair (MTTR).

Security metric:
- Average time to breach a security barrier.

Stability metric:
- Implemented degree of error tolerance for potential failures.

Usability metrics:
- Average time needed to learn how to use the system.
- Average time needed to perform a task.
- Average number of commands to perform a task.
- Response time.

Reusability metrics:
- Number of independent components as a function of the number of separable functions.
- Percentage of non-system-specific module implementations.

Evolvability metric:
- Fraction of system components that are without constraints when extended up to 150[17] per cent of the current capacity or functionality extent, as a function of the total current system extent.

Maintainability metric:
- Effort of system maintenance as a percentage of the initial development effort.

Once critical requirements and their ratings have been defined, processes for how the critical requirements shall be managed should be established and implemented within the monitoring environment.

Note that the accomplished numerical values are system specific and only comparable within the domain of the system under consideration. Using this approach the overall improvements can easily be observed and assessed.

2.5.1.5 Overall dependability evaluation

As presented above, each attribute is characterized by a number of criteria and each criterion is assigned a related metric expression. When evaluating dependability attributes of a system, one can use the expression:

$$D_a = \sum_{i=1}^{M} c_i m_i \quad [Eq.2.22]$$

where:

---

[17] This is an accepted number for purpose of the definition, and the percentage can be changed as long as consistency is perserved.

- c: the coefficient of the criterion.
- i: the criterion index.
- M: number of attributes belonging to the criterion.
- m: value based on metric definition.
- a: attribute.

The (intrinsic part of) total dependability is then given by:

$$D_{tot} = \sum_{a=1}^{N} D_a \quad [Eq.\,2.23]$$

where:
- a: attribute index.
- N: number of attributes.

2.5.1.6 Requirements specification as a prerequisite

System requirements should be the foundation from which dependability is measured. Lack of conformance to requirements is lack of dependability. Thus, requirements should be specified, measured and assessed throughout the whole system development process. This process can be summarized into the following activities:
- Formulation: the derivation of software measures and metrics that are appropriate for representation of software that is being considered.
- Collection: the mechanism used to accumulate data required to derive the formulated metrics.
- Analysis: the computation of metrics and the application of mathematical tools.
- Interpretation: the evaluation of metrics results in an effort to gain insight of the quality of representation.
- Feedback: recommendations derived from the interpretation of technical metrics.

It is not surprising that requirements errors constitute one of the major problem categories in software development. A high percentage of all software defects are requirements errors, which are demanding and often impossible to detect by applying fault tolerance techniques.

Another view of software dependability can be that of process quality versus end-product quality. From customer requirements to the delivery of the software products, the development process is iterative and often involves a series of stages, each with feedback paths. Each stage results in an intermediate deliverable with certain dependability attributes.

To improve dependability during development, we need models of the development process and within the process we need to select and deploy specific methods and approaches and employ proper tools and technologies. We need measures of characteristics and dependability attributes of the product, as well as the development process. One of the means is the developed framework which stresses the product dependability.

2.5.2 A dependability cost-benefit model

Reaching a certain dependability level and at the same time finding the least expensive way of achieving it can be viewed as an optimization problem, as shown in figure 2.5 below.

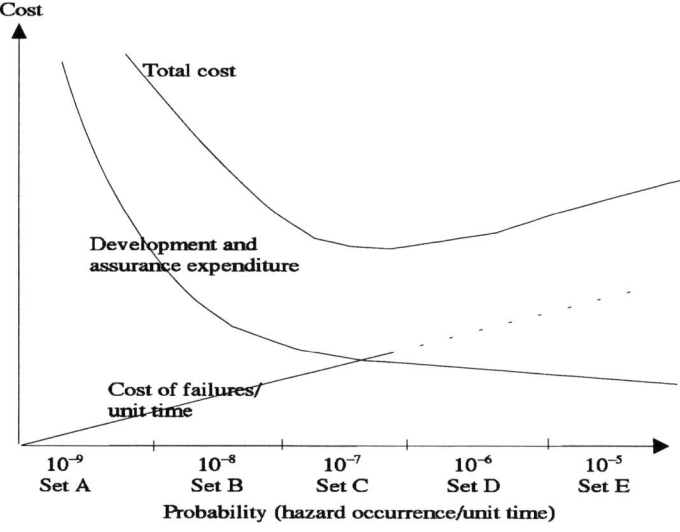

Figure 2.5: Proposed cost-benefit model

The model seeks to find the minimum of the sum of the two parameters, (1) the total cost of development and assurance expenditure and (1) the cost of failures per unit time, that is, the cost of failures per unit time plus the cost of development and assurance. The question is how far to the right one should go and how it can be done. A missing component in the evaluation is revision (see definition above) which is substantially reduced for the assumed high initial development and assurance costs.

The model should associate techniques with error types, application domains and other items which need to be considered relative to the supplier's environment. One suggestion is to associate a probability of failure with a set of techniques as indicated in figure 2.5.

Further development of the model requires a collection of data on failures of systems, types of techniques for development and assurance and the errors they prevented or discovered, and the costs associated with the failures and successes. Cost effectiveness is treated in detail in [Boehm 1981], which is an outstanding reference on the topic.

The cost of dependable design will depend on the type of software and requirements. In [Marciniak 1994] a quantifying method has been deduced giving cost of fault-tolerant software with respect to the cost of non-fault-tolerant software. The average relationship between the two figures for the various fault tolerance methods varied from 1.75 to 225.

When performing a cost-benefit analysis of dependability measures, cost should be defined as the resources required to produce it, while benefits take the form of cost savings, cost avoidance, improved operational performance and "intangibles". Examples of benefits include:
- Improved information.
- More flexible production.
- Reduced number of mistakes.

There are three issues of perspective in any cost-benefit analysis: the statement of purpose of the analysis, the time period considered by the analysis, and the criteria of the analysis.

A value should be assigned to each cost and benefit, followed by establishing a discount rate[18] and calculating the present value of the alternatives. Present value compares the long-range payoffs of alternatives by showing net time-adjusted benefits over time-adjusted costs.

Uncertainties can arise from incomplete identification of alternatives, cost accounting, assigning benefits, special system characteristics, the cost of analysis itself, as well as social issues.

A break-even analysis can indicate a minimum value of intangible benefits that will make it possible for a project to survive. Break-even analysis is often applied where costs are known but benefits are unclear.

System characteristics such as accuracy, response time, security, reliability and flexibility, can significantly affect costs and benefits of an information system relative to a task and the user of an analysis must be aware of the analytic shortcomings. More on the topic can be found in [Boehm 1981].

2.5.2.1 Cost of failures

The cost of a failure is both a function of the fault that causes it and of the situation in which the failure occurs.

$$c(f) = c(f,b) * p_b(t) \quad [Eq. 2.24]$$

where:
c(f,b) = cost of failure f occurring in situation b.
$p_b(t)$ = probability of the situation b at time t.

Since the situations occur in context of an operational profile, cost due to the occurrence of any particular failure is a time based function related to the operational profiles.

---

18 Establishing a discount rate means determining the "time value" of the money invested in the project.

2.5.3 Total Quality Management

Total Quality Management (TQM) is another method to control and improve the system development process by integrating it with the rest of the organizational structure and activities. Numerous sources are available on the topic, examples include [Oakland 1989], [Arthur 1993], [NATO 1984] and [Feiganbaum 1983].

Total in the context of TQM is interpreted meaning the involvement of everything and everyone in continuous improvement. [ISO8402 1986] defines **quality** as:

"The totality of features and characteristics of a product or service that bears on its ability to satisfy stated or implied needs."

This definition provides the degree of objectivity that is essential for TQM and recognizes the problem that requirements are not always well articulated by including the reference to implied needs.

Management in a quality sense provides planning, measurement and control.

Assets of the organization in question are divided into three categories ("the three P's"):
- Process: methods used to sustain continuous improvement.
- Product: all outputs from processes.
- People: the individuals who operate the process to produce the products.

Thus, the definition of TQM can be formulated as:

The infrastructure, tools, methods and rules which result in increased business success and customer satisfaction by enabling continuous improvements to people, processes and products.

TQM is considered as a means to
- Prevent problems occurring.
- Reduce costs.

- Pro-actively manage change.
- Meet customer requirements.
- Increase customer satisfaction.
- Remain competitive.

The operation of a TQM gives added value by providing a framework for the implementation of improvements. While implementing the operation, a loop consisting of the following four stages is repeated:
- Operate.
- Measure.
- Analyze.
- Improve.

This is applied to each of the three P's presented above.

A prerequisite to the implementation of TQM is the establishment of sound project management based on the good business practice of effective planning, measurement and control. The operation of a TQM system gives added value by providing a framework for the implementation of improvements. There needs to be a direct relationship between quality assurance activities in the different life-cycle phases.

To achieve optimal results, the system dependability framework should be applied as an integral part of TQM. This is the only way to ensure the value and quality are maximized, resources fully explored and all the expectations taken into account.

2.5.4 The general methodology deduction

The metrics provide actual indication of the system dependability and an evaluation and assessment mechanism. The objective of a general methodology is to provide a complete implementation scheme for identifying dependability goals, establishing required attributes (factors, recall the framework definition above) and identifying measurements to assess the attainment of these goals.

The approach starts by stating the purpose of the system defining the system borders, identifying the stakeholders and using the factors to identify dependability requirements of the stakeholders.

Each system has unique requirements affected by the type of application, expected life-cycle, risk of use, performance requirements, etc. The stakeholder must evaluate these characteristics and identify which dependability factors are important to emphasize or specify within the context of the development methodology. Table 2 below provides a simplified guidance for selection of important dependability factors.

Stakeholders' requirement/system characteristic	Related dependability factors
Human lives effected	Safety, correctness, reliability, traceability
Real-time application	Correctness, reliability, efficiency
Business critical system	Correctness, reliability, security,
Classified/private data processing	Security
Interrelated with other systems	Interoperability
Hazardous material handling	Correctness, reliability, interoperability
Long life-cycle	Maintainability, flexibility, testability, portability, reusability, evolvability
Continuously changing regulations	Flexibility
Specific user qualifications	Usability, flexibility
Continuous operation	Reliability, maintainability
On-line usage	Correctness, reliability, efficiency, usability, maintainability
Changing environment	Flexibility, evolvability

Table 2: Guidance for selection of important dependability factors

Once the important factors are identified, they are then specified as requirements of the system development. This specification is done by including them as system requirements, providing their definition, identifying supporting criteria and providing measurements to assess their attainment. A possible process is illustrated in table 3. Application of dependability factors should be included in requests for proposals, statements of work, system specifications, software contracts, design documents, test plans, etc.

Stage number	Goal	Directions	Guidelines
1	Determine dependability attributes.	• Clarify the business model objectives and constraints. • Characterize system mission process. • Identify all stakeholders and their requirements. • Identify related services and functions. • Define dependability attributes. • Relate stakeholders' requirements to the dependability attributes.	• Select applicable dependability attributes. • Determine system goals and dependability levels. • Specify them as system requirements.
2	Evaluate dependability attributes and the related criteria. Asses development methodology and life-cycle benefits.	• Assess attribute interrelationships. • Analyze development methodology with respect to the dependability factors. • Conduct feasibility and cost estimations; review costs to develop versus life-cycle benefits.	• Focus on only selected, key dependability attributes. • Relate the definitions of the dependability attributes to the development process.
3	Plan for dependability achievement.	• Allocate attributes to software services in the system. • Carry out a top-to-bottom risk assessment.	• Require dependability levels and attributes during assessment and development.
4	Plan for dependability monitoring.	• Identify criteria and metrics. • Develop appropriate programming standards. • Identify needed audits. • Identify metric collecting tools and approaches. • Develop the test, monitoring and maintenance plans. • Establish metric reporting.	• Identify metrics. • Identify reporting and monitoring approach.

Table 3: Dependability factor specification process

The dependability factors and the associated metrics are contractually included in the following ways:
- As one of the determinants of incentive fees.
- As a part of software quality assurance program.
- Embedded in the software development process.
- As a part of maintainability and reliability demonstration.
- As checklists to be addressed at each formal review.
- As part of the acceptance criteria.

Traceability of the specified goals throughout the development to demonstrable acceptance criteria should be a goal of all software development efforts.

The use of the dependability attributes and associated measurements throughout the life-cycle of a software system and as an organizational process standard, provides the basis for continuous improvement and also facilitates software being an integral part of an organization's Total Quality Management (see TQM above) process. An example of a powerful supporting tool to control TQM is the Balanced Scorecard.

As data are collected across projects within an organization, the process and measurements can also be used as the basis for risk assessment and cost estimation. An excellent resource on the topic of cost analysis and estimations is [Boehm 1981]. The dependability factors support the identifications of risk areas. The measurements provide the mechanism for monitoring progress toward migrating those risks.

2.6 Dependability achievement and measurement

The rest of the chapter focuses on the different fault classification techniques and presents some of the methods available for dependability achievement and assessment.

2.6.1 Dependability means

The development of a dependable computing system calls for the

combined utilization of a set of methods which can be classed into:
- Fault prevention: how to prevent fault occurrence or introduction. Fault prevention is divided into:
  - Fault avoidance. Techniques such as rigorous or formal specification of requirements and the use of proven design methodologies are used to limit the introduction of errors into programs. Typically, specifications are inconsistent, ambiguous, incomplete or do not describe accurately the intent of the system.
  - Fault removal: how to reduce the presence of faults. Fault removal uses code reviews and system testing to detect faults and remove them.
- Fault tolerance: how to ensure a service capable of fulfilling the systems function in the presence of faults.
- Fault forecasting: how to estimate the present number, future incidence and consequences of faults.

It is a combined utilization of the methods from the above, preferably at each step under system development, that can best lead to a dependable computing system.

Given a correct specification, faults can still occur because of implementation mistakes. Such program errors are found by conventional debugging and, where possible, through program proving. However, algorithms may still be incorrect, the different possible types of failures that a component can experience may not be known and the interactions between the software and its environment are almost never predictable in total.

A number of techniques has been adopted in application of each method. The dependability level will result as a compromise between the different stakeholders' requirements and the available resources.

2.6.2 Dependability control process

In large, dynamic real-time computer systems, it is frequently most cost effective to employ different software performance and reliability techniques at different levels of granularity, at different times, or within different subsystems. These techniques include regulation of redundancy and resource allocation, multiversion and multipath execution, adjustments of program attributes and others. Software that may be adapted to meet varying requirements offers a solution.

Dependability control process encompasses achievement and assessment methods as the main aspects. The sections below discuss each one of the two separately.

2.6.3 Methods for dependability achievement

Dependability achievement process relies on a number of well known methods. The most central ones will be mentioned below, while a new approach related to uncertainty handling will be proposed in chapter 3.

Fault avoidance measures consist of the conventional means for ensuring the correct behaviour of any given system purely by preventing the introduction of faults during the development process. In the analysis or design of any particular subsystem, fault avoidance relies fully on the correct behaviour of the rest of the system. The implementation of fault avoidance needs to be reflective to avoid the fault avoidance software causing problems which in turn cause the activation of fault avoidance software causing an infinite regression and inevitable failure of the system.

Fault tolerant software is software that is designed to work despite defects in itself. Fault tolerance is always achieved by some type of redundancy:
- Time redundancy: achieved by the use of recovery blocks and timeout blocks.
- Software redundancy: achieved by the use of information redundancy and multiple computations.
- Hardware redundancy: achieved by the use of passive and active replications.

Redundancy can either be static or dynamic. Static redundancy duplicates components that are used regardless of whether a fault has occurred or not. In dynamic redundancy, the redundant components are used only when a fault has been detected.

The most common means of achieving redundancy are:
- N-version programming; large granularity and full failure suppression capability.
- Recovery blocks; small granularity and full failure suppression capability.
- Software audits; small granularity and partial failure suppression capability.
- Software supervision; large granularity and partial failure suppression capability.

In addition timeout blocks and replications can be used.

Systems can be grouped by the degree of service provided:
- Full fault tolerance. No loss of service in the presence of errors.
- Graceful degradation. System continues to operate, but with some level of service degradation, until the system either recovers or is repaired.
- Fail safe. System ensures its integrity but stops delivering service.

[Son 1995] defines five levels of fault tolerance in RTCSs (Real Time Control Systems), as shown in table 4.

Degree	Assumable damages	Recovery capabilities
4	No loss of visible actions (i.e., output actions or database update actions)	Action-level fault tolerance (recovery of an interrupted visible action)
3	Loss of one or more visible actions	Slow recovery of a service function (no loss of hardware)
2	Loss of one or more service actions	Partial recovery of hardware (service degradation)
1	Loss of all but a core set of critical service actions	Minimum recovery of core hardware (minimum critical services)
0	Loss of critical service	No fault tolerance

Table 4: Degrees of fault tolerance

For a more detailed introduction into the presented topics, it is referred to for example [Nissanke 1997], [Son 1995], [Pham 1992] or [Krishna 1997].

Recovery and correction involve somehow putting the system in a consistent state, correcting and isolating the error if possible so that the fault does not immediately recur and continuing or repeating execution. Two standard approaches to fault recovery are forward recovery and backward recovery. In the latter one, system states are stored at frequent intervals; on an error or abort, the state is "rolled back" to the most recent checkpoint and the computation is repeated. This technique is not always possible to use in real-time applications.

For forward recovery, a consistent future state is determined, the system is forced or placed into the state and execution is resumed from that point. If stored, operational history of the system can be used to trace the correct state corresponding to the current conditions. Typically, forward recovery time is more predictable and faster that the time for rollback. In both approaches to recovery, some non-automatic intervention may be necessary in order to isolate, repair or determine the cause of the fault and recover.

Exception handling is also an attractive mechanism for implementing fault tolerant software.

The recovery block approach is similar to N-version programming in that several versions of software are used. It differs in that additional versions are used only if the current version is believed to have produced an incorrect result. The utility of the recovery block technique depends on the acceptance test by which acceptability of the result is verified. In some cases, acceptance tests can be difficult to develop and may involve an algorithm of sizable complexity, subject to faults as well.

In case of software audits, software data errors are detected and corrected by means of audit programs. These audit programs consist of additional software which has access to the main program's data structures. Typically, audit programs execute at a lower priority than the main program and only periodically check data structures for errors. One of the primary disadvantages of audit programs is that they detect only a known or limited set of errors. Another problem is that the audit programs themselves may contain faults and thus have potential to reduce the overall software dependability rather than improve it.

Software supervision refers to an approach which detects failures based on target system specifications. The target system receives inputs and generates outputs from and to its environment, respectively. The supervisor monitors these input and output signals based on the target system specifications and determines if they constitute valid behaviour. Supervisor consists of an enhanced executable specification of the target system derived from the target system specification. The function of the supervisor is to compare the inputs and outputs to and from the target system with the behaviour specified by the target system's specification.

Software supervision differs from other approaches in that the failures are detected based on a system's specifications. The advantage is that several versions of identical software need not to be produced and therefore the cost of developing and maintaining additional code is less for software supervision compared to others. Furthermore, supervisor is able to detect a much broader spectrum of failures than software audits since no assumptions need to be made about failure modes of the target system. The disadvantage of this technique is that failure retraction is difficult and that specification is assumed to be correct. For further consideration of the topic of run-time monitoring, see chapter 6.

The most remarkable example of software design with self-checking capability is provided by software fault-tolerance, defensive programming, and such (including, for example, executable assertions with exception handling, recovery blocks, N-version or self-checking programming, use of robust data structures and audit programs) which improves both testability and robustness. With N-version programming, for instance, if a program is built as a combination of three versions derived from the same specifications (and a comparator-voter), any failure of only one of the versions becomes an internal error of the program, easily detectable under test for the purpose of revealing faults but not causing the failure of the program, because the voting detects and masks it. This approach assumes correctness and consistency of the requirement specifications and involves high cost associated with development and maintenance of N versions of software.

Unlike hardware where new failures may be introduced due to the age or influence from the environment, most of the failures in software systems originate from the design process. [Torstendahl, 1997] in the article on Open Telecom Platform (OTP) in Erlang[19] introduces a different concept:

"By means of careful system design, and by applying the 90/10 rule (fine-tune the 10 % of Erlang code that occupies 90 % of processing time), it is possible to obtain good run-time performance from Erlang."

A detailed approach into software quality assurance during each of the system life-cycle phases has been given by [Schulmeyer, McManus 1998][20] and [Peng, Wallace 1993][21].

2.6.4 Methods for dependability assessment

A number of methods for dependability assessment of a (sub-system) are already in use. Two of the best known ones, Markov Models and Petri Nets, will be briefly outlined in this section.

Fault trees are often used in analysis. They point out which combinations of conditions or sequence of events lead to a failure. In the case of real-time systems, the inclusion of time is useful.

Although dependability data are needed for components, one is usually concerned with systems of components (or even systems of systems). Methods to calculate dependability are based on the principle of current division. Examples of calculations for some common systems are given in figure 2.6 below.

---

19 See appendix B.
20 This constitutes an excellent reference to the topics of system quality, including definitions, formal methods, quality achievement, measurement and assurance, supported by numerous examples.
21 Approaches application of all the three analysis techniques at each system life-cycle phase.

Design Guidelines for a Monitoring Environment Concerning Distributed Real-Time Systems

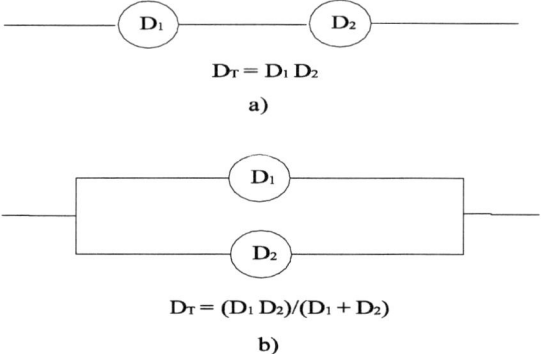

Figure 2.6: Dependability calculations for systems of systems

Markov models are used to model systems that can be described as discrete states with probabilities for instantaneous transitions between the states. Markov models are especially useful for finding the frequencies the different states will be visited and the average time the system will spend on each.

However, Markov models increase very rapidly in size, making analytical solutions hard to find. Engineering approximations and Monte Carlo simulations can be used to solve these.

The Petri net theory offers important advantages to apply it in software design and verification:
- Petri net is a model incorporating elements for a structural as well as a behavioural description of parallel systems.
- Graphical net representation results in a high degree of transparency even for large systems.
- The local process is modeled by the flow of tokens through the net.
- Petri net can be adapted to a special problem class by problem-oriented interpretation of the net elements.
- There are algorithms for a computer-aided analysis and simulation of Petri nets for several net types.

A Petri net is a graphical and mathematical modeling tool. It consists of places, transitions and arcs that connect them. Input arcs connect places with transitions, while output arcs start at a transition and end at a place.

There are other types of arcs, e.g. inhibitor arcs. Places can contain tokens; the current state of the modeled system (the marking) is given by the number and type (if the tokens are distinguishable) of tokens in each place. Transitions are active components. They model activities which can occur (the transition fires), thus changing the state of the system (the marking of the Petri net). Transitions are only allowed to fire if they are enabled, which means that all the preconditions for the activity must be fulfilled (there are enough tokens available in the input places). When the transition fires, it removes tokens from its input places and adds some at all of its output places. The number of tokens removed / added depends on the cardinality of each arc. [Petri Nets]

Petri nets are suitable for an efficient description of both the control and data flow of programs. These models cannot however be analyzed for verification directly and its simulation is insufficient for a complete verification.

The interactive firing of transitions in subsequent markings is called a token game. Petri nets are a promising tool for describing and studying systems that are characterized as being concurrent, asynchronous, distributed, parallel, nondeterministic, and/or stochastic. As a graphical tool, Petri nets can be used as a visual-communication aid similar to flow charts, block diagrams and networks. In addition, tokens are used in these nets to simulate the dynamic and concurrent activities of systems. As a mathematical tool, it is possible to set up state equations, algebraic equations and other mathematical models governing the behavior of systems.

To study performance and dependability issues of systems it is necessary to include a timing concept into the model. There are several possibilities to do this for a Petri net. However, the most common way is to associate a firing delay with each transition. This delay specifies the time that the transition has to be enabled, before it can actually fire. If the delay is a random distribution function, the resulting net class is called a stochastic Petri net.

Different types of transitions can be distinguished depending on their associated delay, for instance immediate transitions (no delay), exponential transitions (delay is an exponential distribution) and deterministic transitions (delay is fixed).

2.7 Summary

The type of system will determine which dependability attributes will be crucial for that system. The ratings and metrics deduced are intended for general use and their adjustment may be desired in certain, special-purpose systems.

The general methodology in section 2.5.4 provides guidelines for framework application in relation to cost-benefit approach and Total Quality Management.

Means of achieving dependability and measurement under the respective life-cycle stages are outlined with emphasis to real-time systems.

Finally, the dependability requirements control process has been considered, including a combined outline-deduction approach to achievement and assessment methods.

The chapter gives the necessary definitions and serves as the background for the later approach.

Chapter 3: Risk analysis and treatment

> "Experience is that marvelous thing that enables you to
> recognize a mistake when you make it again."
> - **F. P. Jones**

3.1 Introduction

This chapter provides a method for risk treatment along the different system life-cycle phases and proposes a framework for risk and vulnerability analysis, which is to be embedded into the monitoring environment.

In spite of current error-prevention processes, errors will tend to occur during software development, operation, revision and transition. Hence, there is a need for error analysis, including the activities of preventing and detecting errors, collecting and recording error data, analyzing and removing single errors and analyzing collective error data to remove classes of errors. The collective error data may be used with statistical process control (SPC)[22] techniques to improve the system and the development process. The second part of the chapter presents a different framework for error handling and recommends collection of error data into a knowledge database for integration with monitoring environment and use by developers in several projects.

3.2 Integrity definition

The notion of integrity assumes a number of minimum system features:
- Lack of impairedness.
- Soundness.
- Completeness.
- Trustworthiness.
- Correctness.
- Uprightness, rectitude.

---

22 See section 3.4

- Freedom from corrupting influence or motive, used especially with reference to fulfillment of contracts.

For the purpose of this document, integrity is defined as a collective term for the characteristics above. Integrity is concerned with the design-related aspects of systems containing both software and hardware. Further, software integrity ensures containment and confinement of risk exposure in software.

Integrity is associated with risk containment. Risk is defined as the combination of the frequency or probability of a system event and the consequence of that system event[23]. Since risk observes no boundaries, it could appear at any level of the system hierarchy. Risk applies to hardware, software or the combination of both, as well as to the system users and surroundings.

System integrity level is defined as the assigned risk associated with the system operation which is to be contained. The procedure for determining risks associated with the potential system events includes evaluation of the system exposure to each risk dimension and assessing whether the risks are tolerable.

The integrity level can be seen as a "negotiated" containment of risk. An integrity target should be mutually established taking into consideration all the necessary aspects (service, cost, security, standards etc.). The respective integrity level is a numerical expression of the policy in terms of the tolerability of risks from an identified system event perspective.

Risk can not be contained in the software alone, since software must operate in the system as a part of its functions. Risk should be addressed from a system perspective to determine its exposure and the means of containing it. The process for assignment of software integrity levels is associated with the software when used in a system for specific application. This is best suited for a top-down process. The software integrity levels provide a method of ranking software based upon a system risk analysis, and also allow assignments of suitable development and qualification methods to each level.

---

23 System event is used as a synonym to a system state carrying a certain risk level.

The integrity level requirements can be expressed using the dependability attribute ratings. Figure 2.6 illustrates how the evaluation on system level can be expressed from the component-based values for each attribute. Note that importance of the different attributes may vary in the overall dependability evaluation. Therefore, each attribute should be assigned a coefficient which is to be used during conversion of the system-based attribute values into the total dependability value of the system.

3.2.1 Integrity metrics deduction

Among main objectives of this chapter is to deduce a general metric expression for integrity that can be employed by a design process. Depending on the current design level, the metric will be deployed on separate components or on the system under integrity testing, which is an iterative process.

3.2.1.1 Component-based approach

For the purpose of a more trustworthy system integrity evaluation, it is proposed to distinguish between component-based and system-based integrity assessment. The overall system-based integrity analysis should rely on the corresponding component-based one, assuming a bottom-up design.

How the component-based calculations should be related to the system-based ones is presented in section 2.6.4. The analysis process should operate on several levels, each one corresponding to the design (or system life-cycle) level in question. Note that the formulations assume risk analysis to be conducted before starting on design and integrity analysis.

Being composed of several criteria, the integrity metric should include each criterion separately. The metric is therefore expressed in form of an array of criterion expressions.

Integrity metric on component level:

$$Integrity = \frac{1}{4}\left(\frac{\sum_{i=1}^{N}W_{ispm}}{\sum_{j=1}^{M}W_{icsi}}; \frac{\sum_{k=1}^{N}W_{icdl}}{\sum_{l=1}^{M}W_{rcdl}}; \frac{\sum_{ii=1}^{N}W_{icse}}{\sum_{jj=1}^{M}W_{rcse}}; \frac{\sum_{kk=1}^{N}W_{eami}}{\sum_{ll=1}^{M}W_{ipcf}}\right) \quad [Eq.3.1]$$

where

- W is the weighting value (the assigned importance level) of the criterion item
- N is the number of criterion items included in the component
- M is the total number of identified criterion items within the component
- i, j, k, l, ii, jj, kk, ll are the the respective criterion item indexes
- ispm: included security protection mechanisms
- icsi: identified component security issues
- icdl: included component detail level
- rcdl: required component detail level
- icse: included component service extent
- rcse: requires component service extent
- eami: error avoidance and exception handling mechanisms included
- identified potential component failures

Each of the fractions is less than or equal to one. Every component is thus assigned a set of four values, each one describing one of the integrity criteria. If integrity of a system of components is to be evaluated, each element within the array is to be treated separately. The total value of each of the consistuting factors is then calculated separately using the method described in section 2.8.2. The value of total system integrity[24] is thus obtained by repeating the process for each factor and involving all the components.

The four most influent integrity variables[25] are included in the definition above:
- Security: this aspect includes protection from system corruption, unauthorized data or system code access, as well as the initial security

---
24 Described by the array of four elements.
25 Also called factors.

of service.
- Detail level: this aspect covers some internal component quality criteria, such as: accuracy, data types, standard fulfillment, understandability, consistency and coherence.
- Service extent: this aspect covers some overall component quality criteria, such as: Interoperability and service domain.
- Error prevention and exception handling: ensures the correctness of the provided service.

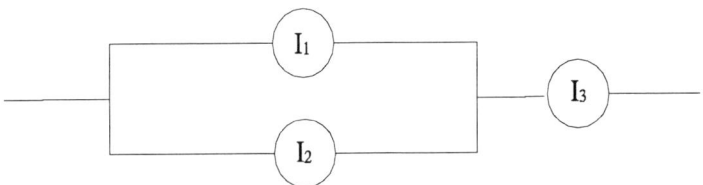

$$I_T = (I_1 + I_2 - I_1 I_2) I_3$$

Total Integrity Array

I_T: Total integrity
I_i:: Integrity array of component "i"
$I_i = (s_i; d_i; se_i; eh_i)$
where
- s_i: security related expression item
- d_i: detail level related expression item
- se_i: service extent related expression item
- eh_i: error handling related expression item

Total integrity is then given by:

$I_T = (I_1 + I_2 - I_1 I_2) I_3 = ((s_1 + s_2 - s_1 s_2)s_3; (d_1 + d_2 - d_1 d_2)d_3; (se_1 + se_2 - se_1 se_2)se_3; (eh_1 + eh_2 - eh_1 eh_2)eh_3)$

The deduced expression is only a general starting point and as such has considerable limitations. Not all the criteria will be considered relevant in all the systems. Their criticalities and definitions will normally vary as well. Note that each one of the factors should be considered independently.

Sometimes, basing integrity evaluations on component-level considerations is impossible or undesirable. One wishes to have a choice and obtain integrity values by starting directly on system level. A system-related approach similar to the component-based one is derived below.

3.2.1.2 System-based approach

The integrity metric on system level can be given by:

$$Integrity = \frac{1}{4} \left(\frac{\sum_{i=1}^{N} W_{isspm}}{\sum_{j=1}^{M} W_{ipssbr}} ; \frac{\sum_{k=1}^{N} W_{issd}}{\sum_{l=1}^{M} W_{rssd}} ; \frac{\sum_{ii=1}^{N} W_{ieam}}{\sum_{jj=1}^{M} W_{ipf}} ; \frac{\sum_{kk=1}^{N} W_{fcc}}{\sum_{ll=1}^{M} W_{ircc}} \right) \quad [Eq.3.2]$$

where

- W is the weighting value (the assigned importance level) of the criterion item
- N is the number of criterion items included in the component
- M is the total number of identified criterion items within the component
- i, j, k, l, ii, jj, kk, ll are the the respective criterion item indexes
- isspm: included system security protection mechanisms
- ipssbr: identified potential system security breach risks
- issd: included system service domain
- rssd: required system service domain
- ieam: included error avoidance mechanisms
- ipf: identified potential failures
- fcc: fulfilled correctness criteria
- ircc: identified random correctness criteria

Also in the case of system integrity assessment, risk analyses are assumed to be performed beforehand. A consistency should be present between the two (component and system) levels of risk assessment and integrity evaluation. Although the two integrity expressions are not linked directly, most of the assessment criteria should be traceable in both directions. The deviations between the values obtained from the two metrics should be limited. This will depend with the preciseness/representativeness of the weightings assigned to the respective criteria items.

In attempt to base the overall system integrity metric on the component metric, one should keep in mind the system specific attributes, such as:
- Component coherence.
- Consistency.
- System security.
- Data accuracy.
- Overall completeness.

For most systems, only certain of these attributes will be critical. The system integrity metric from above opens for their consideration in analysis by introducing the "ircc" variable which can contain criteria from any of the attributes above and assign them the appropriate weightings.

The elementary conditions for integrity achievement during the design stage are:
- Premature decisions are avoided.
- Design is supported by several techniques and they are mutually consistent. Examples of techniques include use of:
  - Pseudocode
  - Data flow diagrams
  - Statecharts
  - Tabular presentations
  - Process diagrams etc.
- Dependability requirements are incorporated into design (preventative measures, degree of redundancy, monitoring, risk analysis, etc.).
- CASE (Computer Aided Software Engineering) tools are used as a supplement, but not as a substitute to development tools and environments. In cases where code optimization is needed, CASE tools offer too generalized solutions and are therefore not desired. Exceptions may occur in cases when detailed detailed specifications have been inserted.

[Wallace, Ippolito, Kuhn 1992] and [Wallace, Ippolito, Kuhn 1994] propose activities towards software integrity achievement throughout system life-cycle. Interested readers are recommender to refer to these sources.

3.3 Life-cycle risk analysis activities

The criticality assessment must be conducted throughout all of the software development phases, implying a strong traceability requirement for hazards that must be avoided or mitigated. This also implies documentation requirements at all life-cycle stages for the hazards being traced. A set of rough dependability requirements for a product must be determined during the initial project planning. Resources required for assuring the desired level of integrity must be identified as well as the level of automation for ensuring the desired integrity level.

At the requirements stage an integrity model should be put in place. This model should reflect the integrity policy defined at the conceptual stage. The model should be sufficiently analyzed to ensure that it accurately reflects the desired type and level of integrity. A preliminary integrity analysis would be performed at this level. The need for isolation of system components critical to the integrity of the system should be decided at the requirements stage as well. Requirements traceability policy and high level test requirements for hazard coverage are also determined at this stage. Test plans and test cases should be constructed and, if necessary, test data generated. Formal methods may be used as required by the integrity policy and model.

At the preliminary design stage, components critical to the integrity of the system should be identified and traced back to the requirements. It is at this stage that the isolation of components critical to the integrity of the system should be enforced. Test cases, test data and test code should again be generated to ensure that the hazards are covered. Standard techniques such as software fault tree analysis are used to identify critical software components and the design should be analyzed to ensure that no new hazards have been introduced as a result of design decisions. Formal methods can be used as required by the integrity policy and model.

At the detailed design level, further analysis should be conducted to evaluate traceability for the identified hazards and to ensure that no new hazards are introduced at this stage. Again, test cases, test data and test code should be generated to ensure the hazards are covered. Formal methods can be used as required by the integrity policy and model.

At the code stage, traceability should be enforced and coding practices adopted to reduce the possibility of hazards being introduced at this stage. Formal methods can be used as required by the integrity policy and model.

Throughout this process, standard software quality assurance activities should be followed. Quality assurance is a prerequisite for high integrity software. Assurance includes checking that the software addresses the hazards and developing tests that "exercise" the software in response to external events that may lead to a hazard. This testing requires that the software addressing the hazards be properly isolated. This isolation also allows for more intensive validation activities, such as use of formal specification or even the formal proof of high integrity properties, to be used.

At the operation and maintenance stage any changes in the environment of the system or in the code itself must be subjected to additional hazard analysis to ensure that the environment changes and/or code changes do not result in unacceptable risk. Records should be kept of the entire development effort in order to build an experience base for the development of future high integrity systems.

The parts or components that cause the highest risk should be handled first. The rationale after the rule to select the highest risk tasks first is to limit the investments in a product that is doomed to fail eventually. Thus, it is better to determine whether the project will succeed or fail as soon as possible by performing the highest- risk tasks first.

3.4 Statistical Process Control

Statistical process control, SPC, is the application of statistical methods to provide the information necessary to continuously control or improve process throughout the entire life-cycle of a product. SPC helps to locate trends, cycles and irregularities within the development process and provide clues about how well the process meets specifications or requirements. It is a tool for measuring and understanding process variation and distinguishing between random inherent variations and significant deviations. This allows correct decisions to be made about whether changes to the process or product are required. Changes over time are recorded, plotted, interpreted and analyzed. The analysis may be based on numerous statistical techniques, such as: Gaussian distribution, Weibull distribution, Beta distribution and Log-Normal distribution (see [Dovich 1990]).

3.5 A risk and vulnerability analysis framework

A detailed and thoroughly-planned risk analysis should be an integral part of each stage of the system life-cycle and is a prerequisite for the application of the ideas and metrics discussed previously.

Considerable contributions have already been made in this field and an entire thesis on the topic could be justified. This section will present the headlines for an alternative approach and give the main guidelines for its construction, application and possible extensions.

The method consists of the following stages:
1. Organization and planning: identify all the stakeholders[26] and their requirements for the system or component, including dependability attributes, service domain, time span and interface. This step involves requirements specification in case of early system development, followed by overall design, detailed design and so forth. I.e., specification of the objectives of the development stage.
2. Define the essential consequence categories as linked to the consequence criticality levels. Examples of consequence categories are specific dependability attributes, people, environment, economy or any aspects considered as essentially influenced by the system and/or its components. Consequence criticality levels give a general

---
26 Stakeholders may be: service user, service supplier, system owner, system seller, system maintainers and system developers. In most cases, the number and definition of stakeholders will differ and the roles may overlap.

description of the expected consequence severity and each one is assigned a corresponding numerical value.

3. Define a set of probability levels based on state occurrence frequencies. These too are given both a qualitative and a quantitative definition.
4. Integrity requirements level: determine the acceptable integrity levels and the determining criteria. This is done by forming a cross-reference table (or graph) of discrete probability levels versus consequence criticality levels for each identified consequence category and specifying the risk acceptance borders within the formed quadrant.
5. Conduct an overall analysis of the system or component and identify the most strategically critical parts. The purpose is to determine the focusing areas during the analysis.
6. Conduct a risk and vulnerability analysis, consisting of:
   - Identification of all potential occurrences[27] as related to the components, functions or service categories[28]. If an occurrence-(component, function or service category) combination is realistic within the component or system under consideration, it is formalized and called a state[29].
   - Assign a probability level to each state.
   - Link possible causes to each identified state. According to [Arthur 1993], there are two causes of variation in software processes that cause problems: common causes and special causes; representing 85 and 15 percent, respectively.
   - For each combination of states and its cause, identify the possible consequences[30] corresponding to the defined consequence categories.
   - Assign the appropriate consequence criticality level to each one of the cause-state-consequence (set) combinations above.
   - Plot the state coordinates with their respective probability-consequence criticality values on the risk graph as described under

---

27 "Occurrence" is used in this context as a collective term for risks, faults, hazards, failures or any undesired conditions. An occurrence may be an operation, behaviour, transaction or exception.
28 Occurrences should be linked to the related components, functions or service categories which also are to be identified and defined for the current life-cycle stage and the analysis level.
29 A state consists of an occurrence-function combination and is the basis for further analysis.
30 For implementation reasons and correct storage of the system related knowledge, independent sets of consequence lists in distinct situations should be distinguished.

point 4 in order to observe the risk conditions.
- For each cause-state-consequence set, assign the appropriate set of actions to be undertaken. The actions can be divided in two categories:
  - preventative: to avoid the identified condition.
  - corrective: to perform changes to the system in order to reverse it to the state it was in before initiation of the condition (and it's consequences).
- Refine the analysis by iterating the steps within point 6.
7. Implementation and run-time supervision of the actions.

3.6 Guidelines for framework application

A computer aided tool should be used to conduct the analysis in order to ensure the correct methodology and keep track of all the experiences and statistics. The structure presented above can be converted into a relational model. This should develop into a knowledge database, which in the long term would be large enough to be embedded in the monitoring environment, enabling it to predict risks and take the appropriate actions (as specified in the database) during the system operation. This would improve system availability, correctness and a number of other attributes.

Auditors my use the information in the database to identify the most error-prone features of specific high integrity systems and may ensure that their audits examine these features carefully. The auditors my use the data to identify the acceptance limits on different aspects of a high integrity system. Note however that, while error analysis at all phases are important, there is no better time in terms of cost-benefit to conduct error analysis than during the software requirements phase.

If used during system development stages, the framework should be an integral part of the system development and be taken into account during system design. A significant benefit from the implementation would be more-structured analysis, experience collection, system integration, real-time operation and quantification of the methodology.

Most of the applications will require operation in real time using a minimum of system resources. A non-real-time option of the risk assessment tool should also be available. In both cases, the tool will share system resources with the main application and preferably be separated from the monitoring program, as the latter one is not supposed to interfere with the main application, while the risk assessment tool should be allowed to undertake actions and do changes on the target application.

The nature of the framework and its hierarchical perspective is well suited for the implementation of the software aided tool as a database, integrating the proposed aspects with statistical methods, previously collected data, risk calculations and the rest of the system. The advantage of viewing data as a relation is that one can use relational languages to examine the data. A drawback is that such an approach imposes the issued of distributed real-time databases[31].

3.7 Summary

Integrity is closely linked to risk containment. Risk analysis should be undertaken at each life-cycle stage, implying a strong traceability requirement for hazards that must be avoided or mitigated. This can be supported by statistical process control methods.

The deduced risk and vulnerability framework can be used as an integrated approach to risk containment and integrity enhancement.

A computer aided tool should be used to conduct the analysis. This ensures the correct methodology is used and keeps track of all the experiences and statistics. This corresponds to a knowledge database, which in the long term would be large enough to be embedded in the system, enabling it to predict risks and take the appropriate actions (as specified in the database) during the system operation.

---

31 See section 5.5.

Chapter 4: Real-time system considerations

"Real time is a level of computer responsiveness that a user senses as sufficiently immediate or that enables the computer to keep up with some external process."
John Huntington

4.1 Introduction

The timing requirements in a control system are directly linked to its correctness and therefore crucial. The aim of this chapter is to briefly outline the main issues related to timing requirements, give recommendations on appropriate measures that can be taken during the different life-cycle stages, reveal the methods available to fulfill the requirements, as well as to discuss the issues of real-time transactions and performance evaluation.

4.2 Real-time requirements

The four fundamental issues that must be considered when developing real-time systems of any character (that is, regardless of the type of timing requirements) are:
- The view of processes.
- The means of communication.
- The method of synchronization.
- Data consistency.

The objective is to manage these problems, make the results predictable and provide satisfactory service as well as ensure maintainability and extendibility of the system. Most programming languages have resources for dealing with these issues. Examples include Erlang and Ada.

The system architecture needs to be defined early on in order to provide for proper allocations of requirements and timing budgets between hardware and software. Early rapid prototyping is recommended for large, complex, state-of-the-art, real-time programs to validate the overall system architecture and to identify critical functions, interfaces and problem areas as soon as possible. Modeling and analysis help to evaluate the impact of the selected hardware and software. Since hardware is difficult to undo later on, software may receive the brunt of unplanned, downstream changes to account for unforeseen oversights in hardware selection. Late changes on software tend to increase software complexity which may adversely impact real-time performance. Peer inspections, reviews, audits and documentation play a significant role in the success of real-time system software. Some recommendations are listed up below.

Requirements

- Review real-time software requirements.
- Evaluate requirements for concurrent processing and interrupt handling.
- Evaluate the software for its ability to meet real-time processing needs.
- Evaluate requirements establishing "not-to-exceed" timing estimates for each function.
- Promote extensive analysis and tradeoff studies to optimize timing allocations.
- Promote use of rapid prototyping.
- Promote tighter controls on the front end of the life-cycle.
- Model real-time software reliability and provide early predictions.

Design

- Monitor the approved list of "not-to-exceed" timing estimates to assure they are not being exceeded.
- Promote peer inspections of design components to assure the intended capabilities of the real-time system.
- Monitor cyclomatic complexity of design modules to stay within tolerable limits.
- Optimize concurrent and interrupt processing.
- Track results of rapid prototyping for the optimization of requirements criteria.

- Investigate shortcomings in hardware for the impact of unplanned additional changes of software.

Implementation

- Monitor the approved list of "not-to-exceed" timing estimates to assure they are not being exceeded.
- Monitor processes that implement concurrent processing schemes.
- Promote peer inspections of code and unit tests.
- Track the impact of software growth and changes on allocated timing budgets for software.

Verification

- Participate in dry runs to assure real-time performance.
- Monitor actual timing results during stand-alone, integration and system level testing.

Operation

- Track real-time performance.
- Track reliability and correctness requirements.
- Perform the necessary analysis, corrective and perfective actions under monitoring and take logs.
- Undertake the appropriate actions on the target system and modifications of the monitoring environment in order to adjust the system to (changed) dependability requirements[32].

Real-time requirements should be documented during the design process by using use-cases in order to make them traceable and verifiable at all system life-cycle stages. Timing and concurrency requirements need to be specified. For systems that interact with the environment, the real-time considerations will normally be made both internally (within the system and at several levels) and externally (between the system and its environment). Typical problems that occur include deadlock, starvation or process racing.

---

32 The change of requirements can come from either changed attributes or dependability level requirements on the existing attributes. Such a situation will, however, interfere with the "revision"-area of dependability framework and be treated accordingly.

In the case of object-oriented design, one process may involve several objects and one object may be involved in several processes. Use-case behaviours can be used to identify and illustrate these. A real-time requirement from a use case can be allocated to an object using interaction diagrams. Parallel processing is illustrated by using interaction diagrams. To handle concurrency and racing, state transition graphs may be used. They can be utilized in detecting erroneous stimuli received at wrong times. This should be designed to get a more fault-tolerant system.

Use of threads may in some cases be an attractive alternative when it comes to the questions of memory management.

Language properties include mutual exclusion, semaphores, monitors, locks, different scheduling algorithms, process priority and so on.

To ensure that timing requirements are met, the rate-monotonic scheduling algorithm (see [Krishna 1997]) can be used under certain conditions. The processes must be independent, periodic and execute under a pre-emptive scheduler. Additionally, the processes must have an upper limit of execution time. The strategy is to set the process priorities in decreasing order of their process execution period. Hence the most frequently executed processes will have the highest priority and less frequently executed processes will have lower priority. [Suri, Walter, Hugue 1995] presents some of the important achievements on scheduling, synchronization and fault tolerance.

4.3 Transactions and concurrency control

Transactions are used to provide sequences of operations that are atomic in the presence of other concurrent transactions and server crashes. Atomicity is achieved by running transactions so that their effects are serially equivalent.

Nested transactions can be formed by structuring transactions from other sub-transactions. Nesting is particularly useful in distributed systems because it allows concurrent execution of subtransactions in separate servers. Nesting also has the advantage of allowing independent recovery of parts of a transaction.

In scheduling an operation in a transaction, three alternative strategies are possible:
- To execute it immediately.
- To delay it.
- To abort it.

In most cases abortion is only used in case of a deadlock. Methods that combine all the three strategies can not suffer from deadlock. Starvation may occur due to repeated aborting of a transaction.

Transaction-based applications have strong requirements for the long life and integrity of the information stored. Atomic commit protocols are used in distributed transactions but they can not be guaranteed to complete within a given time limit. Transactions can be made durable by performing checkpoints and logging in a recovery file, which can be used for recovery when a server is replaced after a crash.

4.4 Performance evaluation in parallel systems

Amdahl's law is considered to be the most fundamental result in parallel systems performance evaluation. Amdahl's law states that if s is the fraction of a computation that must be executed serially, then the speedup of the computation is bounded above by $\frac{1}{s+\frac{(1-s)}{n}}$, where n is the number of processors used. Note that lim of the expression above when n goes to infinity approaches $\frac{1}{s}$. Thus, the effort needs to be directed to the sequential processing rates.

Amdahl's law defines an upper bound on the performance of a parallel computation, relative to its sequential execution time, in terms of a single software parameter (the fraction of sequential computation) and a single hardware parameter (the number of processors).

In experimental evaluation of parallel performance there are two basic requirements:
- The need to specify new problems. The specification can be made in terms of:
  - the characteristics of the system,
  - the structure and parameters of the application program,
  - the stored performance knowledge and
  - the current, empirical performance data.
- The need to conduct performance experiments (including performance measurements, analysis, presentation and modeling) to assess performance behaviour.

4.4.1 Performance observability

Performance observability is the ability to accurately capture, analyze and present information about the performance of a system. Need must be balanced with the cost of obtaining the data. To be observable, events must be measurable by the monitoring system. The selection of instrumentation and data collection tools defines both the granularity and detail of performance data that can be measured. Implementational issues are:
- Timestamp consistency (accuracy and synchronization).
- Trace buffer allocation.
- Tracing of overhead.
- Tracing of I/O.

Techniques to control monitoring overhead dynamically by changing instrumentation during execution can be used to reduce the amount of performance data being captured.

As parallel programs are composed of multiple threads of control, the accuracy of performance characterization depends on some global knowledge of system state. Behavioural models of parallel program execution allow events to be measured independently for each thread of execution and then combined to determine global states. In addition, certain measurements must be made to preserve global integrity of performance data. Thus, parallel program measurement must not only capture thread actions that reflect logical, operational behaviour, but also data that will be used to establish an accurate reference for performance analysis.

4.5 Summary

Real-time issues include communication, synchronization and data consistency. General measures to be taken in addressing them are recommended for each system life cycle stage separately and the main techniques outlined.

Ensuring reliable transactions is required for the long life and integrity of the information stored and main methods for achieving this are presented.

In addition, performance evaluation and main techniques for achieving observability are outlined.

Chapter 5: Distributed systems

"A person with one watch knows what time it is;
a person with two watches is never sure."
[Manber 1989]

5.1 Introduction

The requirements on distributed systems rely upon the ones on real time. This chapter discusses the main issues related to the coming approach on monitoring of distributed real-time systems. Main characteristics are outlined and useful techniques presented. This is followed by a listing up of the requirements and an approach into distributed databases.

5.2 Main issues and characteristics

A distributed system consists of numerous distinct processes running on different processors working towards specified functional requirements. The processors or computers, called nodes[33], may be dispersed geographically, and the distributed processes are coordinated by interprocess communication and synchronization. There may be more than one processor on each distinct node. Distributed systems can be classified as homogenous or heterogeneous, depending on whether the nodes have the same architecture and/or supporting software. Another classification scheme is to distinguish between centralized and decentralized distributed systems. Centralized distributed systems have master-slave or server-client relationships between their distinct computing nodes while decentralized distributed systems have autonomous computing nodes.

Distributed real-time systems (DRTSs) contain characteristics of both distributed and real-time systems. A system may be distributed to improve response time and reliability or the application itself may be distributed. Some characteristics of DRTSs as compared to non-

---
33 A node in this context should be distinguished from an Erlang node, which is a language related term.

distributed real-time systems (non-DRTs) are:
- Continuous operation. The system has to run continuously to maintain normal operation and be ready to take timely action.
- Stringent timing constraints. The correctness is determined not only by the underlying nodes but also by the entire system response.
- Asynchronous process interaction.
- Unpredictable communication delays and race conditions due to geographic dispersion and resource sharing.
- Nondeterministic, nonrepeatable and unpredictable results.
- Global clock reference and global state.
- Multiple threads and process interaction.
- Size of the system due to multiple processes and processors.

Execution of a distributed system can be viewed as a sequence of events that causes transformation in the program's state. The state of a program consists of the local state of each process (including the value of all local variables, the program counter, and the contents of the local stack), and the state of all message channels (i.e., the contents of all messages in transit between processes). An event is any activity that causes a change in program state, such as:
- Execution of a procedure.
- Sending or receiving of a message.
- Process start and end.
- Resource lock and unlock.
- Transaction begin and end.
- Transaction commit and abort.
- Start/end acquisition.
- Time adjustment.
- Directory lookup.
- Security authorization.
- File open/close/access.
- Node failure and repair.
- Communication failure and repair.

During risk analysis[34], interest is in relating specific events to specific changes in state, so as to discover the cause-and-effect relationship between program statements and erroneous states.

---
34 See chapter three.

5.3 Useful techniques

Replication is a well known method of increasing availability. However, guaranteeing consistency while at the same time maintaining a large degree of availability is a very difficult problem. The most trivial algorithm for maintaining consistency is to lock every replica before an update, to update every replica and to unlock each one again. Obviously, this makes availability worse that that of a single copy - every replica must be working in order to make progress. If used, Erlang contains mechanisms for handling this problem.

There is a trade off between availability and consistency. In some cases it is acceptable to sacrifice some availability to achieve absolute consistency, while in other cases some controlled inconsistencies can be allowed to achieve better availability.

A "hint" is a saved result of some operation that is stored away so that carrying out the operation again can be avoided by using the hint. Note however that:
1. A hint may be obsolete.
2. When a wrong hint is used, it will be found out in time (and the hint can be corrected).

Hints are often very easy to use and can result in staggering performance improvements in distributed systems. This makes hints a vital technique in designing and building high performance distributed systems.

Stashing can be used to allow autonomous operation. The word stash was first used by Birell and Schroeder at the 1988 ACM SIGOPS workshop in Cambridge. Stashing is a name for a class of techniques and refers to keeping local copies of key information for use when remote information is not available.

Caching, stashing and using hints are three techniques for improving system operation by avoidance of remote access.

In addition, self-diagnosis and authentication mechanisms should be included. When communication is permitted and service is supported, the origin and legacy of requests should be authenticated. Mechanisms are needed by which whole system components can monitor themselves continuously, actively looking for inconsistencies and taking the necessary actions if problems are detected. The reasoning here is that although software bugs may be inevitable, if they are detected rapidly, the consequences can often be limited. [Mullender, 1993]

A solution to the timing issues is to provide a form of physical clock synchronization based on the exchange of messages containing timestamps, which may contain an external timestamp received from an accurate global (broadcasted) time signal.[35]

In summary, distributed computing offers advantages in its potential for improving system availability and reliability through replication; performance through parallelism; sharing and interoperability through interconnection and flexibility, incremental expansion and scalability through modularity. However, to gain these benefits, one must cope with the issues that distributed computing raises. The interactions between the concurrent processes give rise to issues of non-determinism, contention and synchronization. Component separation and autonomy give rise to issues of partial separation and partial failure. These issues demand that one adapts effective engineering methods and tools.

5.4 Requirements on distributed systems

The construction of distributed systems produces a number of challenges:
- Heterogeneity: they must be constructed from a variety of different networks, operating systems, computer hardware and programming languages. Communication protocols and middleware are means of dealing with this issue.
- Openness: distributed systems should be extensible. The first step is to publish the interfaces of the components, but the integration of components written by different languages is a challenge.
- Security: encryption can be used to provide adequate protection of shared resources and to keep sensitive information secret when it is

---

35 Alternatively, a system of logical clocks, based on the causality relation, can be used to establish a partial ordering of events in the system. This method is not recommended due to its difficulty to prove correctness and because it involves intrusiveness.

transmitted in messages over a network.
- Scalability: a distributed system is scalable if the cost of adding a user is a proportional amount in terms of the resources that must be added.
- Failure handling: each component needs to be aware of the possible ways in which the components it depends on may fail and be designed to deal with each of those failures appropriately.
- Concurrency: the presence of multiple users in a distributed system is a source of concurrent requests to its resources. Each resource must be designed to be safe in a concurrent environment.
- Transparency: the aim is to make certain aspects of distribution invisible to the application programmers so that they need only be concerned with the design of their particular application.

5.5 Distributed databases

The prime fundamental consideration in design of distributed data is that in real-time control systems one can not disassociate the value of data and its time of creation. A distributed computer control system is controlling a process which has temporal characteristics. Database consistency is fundamental and can only be achieved with an eye on the real-time nature of the data. Decisions have to be made according to a temporarily consistent picture. To satisfy both the consistency and real-time constraints, there is a need to integrate synchronization protocols with real-time priority-based scheduling protocols. Database control mechanisms should be integrated with the operating system, because the correct functioning of control mechanisms depends on the services of the underlying operating system. An integrated design reduces the significant overhead of a layered approach during execution[36]. To assure atomicity, a message based communication approach is recommended.

The two basic methods for preserving the integrity of a concurrent distributed database are locking and timestamping. If a locking protocol is used, transactions must take out a lock on an item before being able to read or write to it. In timestamping, transactions are given timestamps; the consistency of the database is preserved by comparing these

---

36 Although an integrated approach is desirable, the system needs to support flexibility which may not be possible in such an approach.

timestamps with the read or write timestamps of the data items which are to be read or written.

Data integrity is in distributed real-time databases conditioned by timing requirements. While mechanisms for data integrity assurance are necessary, their inclusion will degrade system performance. There is obviously a trade off between the two. [Blesa, Zambardino 1990] proved timestamping to be preferred mechanism, as it introduces shorter delays as compared to locking. To increase efficiency, the distributed data should be placed close to processing.

5.5.1 Active database systems

Active database systems support mechanisms that enable them to respond automatically to events that are taking place either inside or outside the database system itself. Active databases are able to observe and react to specific circumstances. The reactive semantics is both centralized and handled in a timely manner. To support the reactive behaviour, the active database is provided with a knowledge model and an execution model (that is, a runtime strategy – equivalent with action specifications in the risk analysis framework). An occurrence may be composite, in which case the action is raised by some combination of primitive or composite events. Several events may occur at the same time, in which case the related actions will need to be prioritized and cooperated.

5.5.2 Requirements

To be suitable for use in a control environment, a DBMS must support both the design and the operation of a control system in such a way that interaction between the two is natural. Some of the aspects include:
- It must be possible to define and manipulate objects with complex structure, and structural change itself must be easy.
- During the design phase there must be support for version maintenance, together with logging and recovery of long transactions.
- The scheduler must give good response to transactions initiated by

unforeseen events without prejudicing deadlines for the synchronous processing of large data volumes.
- The database must be integrated with a distributed real-time operating system, ideally one with a predictive performance model.
- If software products are to be developed, then standards will be needed for languages and data models.

5.6 Summary

Distributed real-time systems (DRTSs) contain characteristics of both distributed and real-time systems. A system may be distributed to improve response time and reliability or the application itself may be distributed.

Distribution imposes issues such as non-determinism, diversity, inconsistent timing and complex synchronization, but can also be advantageous when it comes to the possibilities for replication of data, software and hardware components. Main characteristics of a DRTS are listed up.

The main techniques for addressing the issues of DRTS are presented and include replication, stashing, hints, caching, self-diagnosis, authentication mechanisms and timestamping. This is followed by a generalized listing of requirements on distributed systems.

The issue of distributed databases is important in the approach used in the succeeding chapter and has therefore been considered separately, including an overview of characteristics, methods and requirements.

Chapter 6: A monitoring framework for distributed real-time systems

"Monitor: a software tool or hardware device that operates concurrently with a system or component and supervises, records, analyzes, verifies the operation and provides detailed information about the execution of the system or component."
[Glos 1993]

6.1 Introduction

The tasks associated with the software aspects of a system are to be treated from dependability attribute requirements viewpoint, such that they can be predicted, evaluated and assessed for continuous improvement. This chapter presents an approach to monitoring as a dependability handling tool.

As real-time systems become more sophisticated, the ability of the system to provide dependable and timely service becomes more critical. The unpredictability of the environment and the inability to satisfy design assumptions due to the inherent complexity of systems can cause unexpected conditions or violations of system constraints at run time. A monitoring facility can dynamically acquire the system state information and trigger appropriate action if a constraint is violated. Furthermore, it can also be used to test the simulation of the executable specification before the system is operational or even before it is fully implemented.

Real-time software must respond to the changing environment causing the dependability requirements to be frequently changed. This results in a need for dynamic systems. The software needs to be modified and tuned in real time to maintain its dependability requirements.

Software adaption can be defined as any software modification that changes the attributes of software without affecting other aspects of its functionality. Adaptions are specified by adaption algorithms, which describe the changes to be performed and the circumstances that trigger the adaption.

In contrast to testing, this chapter deals with issues of *observing and controlling the target system in real-time during its operation and therefore aims to concentrate on addressing the operation-area related issues of dependability framework*. Redundant software[37] acts as a supervisor by monitoring inputs and outputs of the target system and checking them against the target systems specification. For a further reading on software, hardware and hybrid run-time monitoring of real-time (distributed) systems, see [Tsai, Yang 1995].

"Past lessons have taught us that non-functional properties cannot be added as an afterthought; they must be at the core of the architecture and protocol designs. Success of integrating real-time methods into open systems thus has the potential of significant social impact." [Stankovic 1996]

6.2 Monitoring of distributed real-time programs

Monitoring of distributed real-time systems must be achieved in order to measure, debug, test and develop systems efficiently. While a key requirement of real-time system monitors is low overhead, the most critical requirement is predictable overhead. Monitoring can be defined as the measurement, collection, processing of information about execution of tasks and dynamic adjustments of the target system in accordance with the (changing) dependability requirements. System characteristics may influence this process.

A real-time target system requires the monitor itself to operate under strict reliability and performance constraints. The reliability constraints require that the monitored system and the monitor continue to operate in the presence of static or dynamic failures. The performance constraints require that the interference caused to the system by the monitor's presence must be predictable, minimal and bounded. In particular, the monitor must not introduce or hide timing errors or any other errors.

---

37 Or hardware, whose role will mostly be abstracted away during the course of this study.

Distribution also imposes constraints on the monitor. Distributed systems lack both global state information and a sense of global time. There is no total ordering defined for events that occur on different nodes. Monitored data must be collected from several sites and integrated to obtain a coherent view of the system.

Monitoring activity can be described as an event-driven activity consisting of event detection and event data collection, which can be implemented with software modules, hardware devices or both (hybrid monitoring approaches), depending on the system's tolerance of monitoring interference.

Software monitors present information in an application oriented manner that is easy to understand and use, compared to the low-level information generated by hardware monitors. Software monitors can easily be replicated and are more flexible, portable, and easier to design and construct than hardware monitors. The disadvantage of software monitors is that they usually share the resources with the monitored system thus impacting on its behaviour.

Hybrid monitors employ the advantages of both hardware and software monitors, while overcoming their inefficiencies. Typical hybrid systems consist of their own independent resources but also share some of the resources with the monitored system. The main advantage of hybrid monitors is that they introduce less intrusion in the monitored system compared with pure software monitors. Hybrid monitors are less portable because of their use of dedicated hardware.

6.3 Run-time software monitoring

In designing real-time systems, one often makes assumptions about the behaviour of the system and its environment. These assumptions are made to deal with the unpredictability of the external environment or to simplify a problem that is otherwise intractable or very hard to solve. The need to perform run-time monitoring is due to:
- The fact that execution environment of most systems is imperfect and the interaction with the external world introduces additional

unpredictability.
- The design assumptions can be violated at run time due to unexpected conditions such as transient overload.
- The application of formal techniques or scheduling algorithms requires assumptions about the underlying system.
- It may not be feasible to verify formally some properties at design time, thus further necessitating run-time checks.

There are a number of monitoring alternatives:
- Combine the monitoring code and the main program code and treat them as a single process model.
- A dual process model, where the monitoring processes run in parallel with the monitored processes.
- A thread-based model, where the monitor processes run in separate threads forming the main application processes, but they can share the same memory space.
- The embedded model, where the monitoring is built into the operating system. The disadvantages of an operating system based approach include: an inability to monitor language dependent emergent-dependability attributes of a process, difficulty supporting user defined monitors, difficulty in monitoring language specific features and difficulty relating low level information back to code, design or requirements.

Typical distributed systems generate large amounts of monitoring information. This results in heavy usage of resources such as CPU and communication bandwidth. Data gathering can be done either by interrupts or by polling.

Run-time monitoring requires the timestamping and recording of relevant event occurrences, analyzing the past history as a computation progresses and providing feedback to the rest of the system. A computation of a real-time system can be viewed as a sequence of event occurrences. Thus, timing properties can be expressed as relationships among event occurrences in a computation. Events denote state changes in a system as seen by the monitoring subsystem. Further, event histories should be used to store the times of a bounded number of previous occurrences of each event. The size of the event history for each event should either be specified by the system designer or determined by examining the assertion to be monitored at run time. Under steady conditions and for less critical components, the monitor needs only be notified upon a state change.

Timing constraints should be monitored. This can be done synchronously or asynchronously.

In synchronous monitoring, the monitor can explicitly check for the satisfiability of a constraint at a particular point in the execution of the program and modify the computation accordingly. This is done by directly manipulating the event histories that are shared by the cooperating tasks. Thus, testing and handling any violation of the constraint is carried out synchronously on the threads of the executing tasks.

Alternatively, in asynchronous monitoring, the constraint is enforced during the entire execution of the program. Thus, testing and handling of exceptions are performed asynchronously. The events generated by the application tasks are sent to the system monitor (a separate task), which is responsible for maintaining the event histories. Whenever an event occurs that may violate the satisfiability of the constraint, the system monitor reevaluates the expression and invokes the appropriate handler if the constraint is no longer satisfiable. The rationale for asynchronous monitoring is that, for certain assertions, it may be impossible to insert a test at a particular point in the program and synchronously check for its satisfiability. Asynchronous monitoring separates the timing concerns from the functional specification of the program.

To minimize intrusion of the monitoring processes into the functional ones, a dual model can be used by implementing one monitoring process for each functional one. Each process will then get its own address space. Another approach is to use a communication protocol which delivers messages in the order they would have been delivered without presence of a monitoring protocol.

6.4 Control theory and neural networks in software monitoring

In his book on neural networks, Skapura dedicates a chapter to control theory and explains the tight links between the two:
"Control theory, the body of mathematics that describes the intersections between a controllable process and the mechanisms used to monitor[38] and correct errors in the process, is one of the oldest disciplines in automation technology. In fact, one of the earliest known applications of an automatic control system dates back to ancient Greece. In 250 BC, a man named Philon developed a float-regulator mechanism to maintain a constant level of fuel oil in an oil lamp. Although simple, Philon's system illustrates some of the fundamental ideas of modern control theory, including the notion of feedback, in which the actual system output is compared to the desired response and the difference between the two is used to alter the system." [Skapura 1996]

Figure 6.1 illustrates block diagrams of the two basic types of automatic control systems in common use today: these are referred to as open-loop and closed-loop systems. Feedback allows the controller to determine if, and by how much, the output is in error. After assessing the state of the system via the feedback signal(s), the controller[39] can make corrective adjustments in the input of the system, thus causing the output to stay within some predetermined tolerance or dependability level.

If one of the inputs to the control system is a signal indicating an error at the output, and the control system operates in a manner that attempts to minimize the error signal, the system is said to be closed-loop or self-adjusting.

Using the principles of feedback and correction, it is possible to construct models of extremely complex processes. From these models, one can supply mathematical tools that enable us to understand the behaviour of the models, and, hence, the nature of the target system.

---

38 The term has a meaning of data acquisition in this context.
39 In this case the monitoring environment.

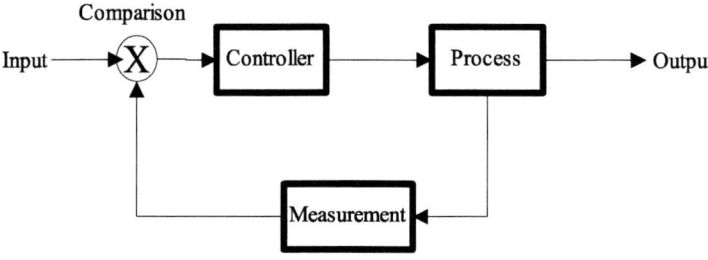

Figure 6.1: Open-loop and closed-loop systems, respectively

Besides being a good prototyping tool, neural networks embedded into control systems, neurocontrollers, can be used to model an application prior to analysis and provide insights to system designer that might otherwise be overlooked. Adaptive networks tend to find their own methods for encoding relationships between system input and output during learning. For a detailed approach into learning generalization and the related theoretical background based on control theory and mathematics, see [Vidyasagar 1997].

In essence neural networks consist of networks of primitive process elements (also called process or computational nodes), as shown in figure 6.2.

The nodes receive inputs x from other nodes in the network or from the outside, which are subsequently weighted and summed. These weighted sums ($w^T x$, also called potentials of the nodes) are then operated by so-called node transfer functions $g(w^T x)$, which map the potentials to smaller domains before passing the output to other nodes or the outside environment of the network.

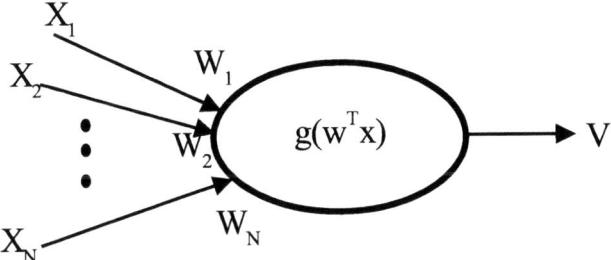

Figure 6.2: Model of a neural network node, with an input vector $X=[x_1,x_2,...,x_N,]^T$ and a weight vector $W=[w_1,w_2,...,w_N,]^T$.

The structure of a basic feed-forward network is shown in figure 6.3. The network has at least an input and an output layer, and possibly one or more hidden layers. Nodes in these layers are connected by means of artificial synapses, each of which is associated with a numerical value or weight. The network is trained by adapting weights on basis of examples of the process.

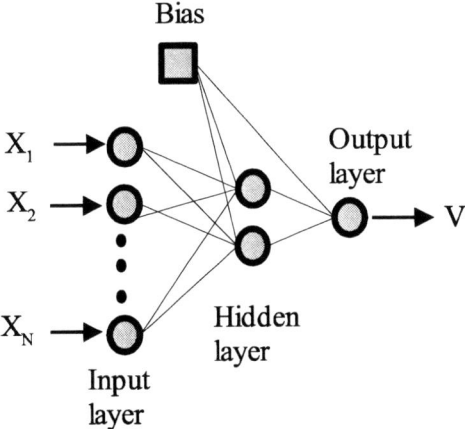

Figure 6.3: Generic structure of a feedforward neural network with a single hidden layer

Computation in the network is normally feed forward and synchronous, i.e., the states of the computational elements in the layers nearest to the input layer of the network are updated before units in successive layers further down in the network. The activation rules of the network determine the way in which the process units are updated and are typically of the form

$$v_i(t+1) = g[u_i(t)] \quad [Eq.6.1]$$

where $u_i(t)$ designates the potential of a process unit at time t, i.e. the difference between the weighted sum of all the inputs to the unit and the unit bias.

$$u_i(t) = \sum j w_{i,j} * V_j(T) - \partial_j \quad [Eq.6.2]$$

The form of the transfer function g may vary but should have a domain smaller than that of the potential of the process unit, such as [0;1] or [-1; 1].

The training of a commonly used back-propagation neural network is an iterative process involving the changing of the weights of the network, typically by means of a gradient descent method, in order to minimize an error criterion, that is

$$w_{i,j}(t+1) = w_{i,j}(t) + delta\, w_{i,j} \quad [Eq.6.3]$$

where

$$delta\, w_{i,j} = -\lambda \partial \mathfrak{I} / \hbar\, w_{i,j} \quad [Eq.6.4]$$

and where λ is the learning rate and $\mathfrak{I}$ the error criterion, i.e.

$$\hbar = \frac{1}{2} \sum j(T_{o,j} - v_{o,j})^2 \quad [Eq.6.5]$$

based on the difference between the desired ($T_{o,j}$) and the actual outputs ($v_{o,j}$) of the unit. Since the error $\mathfrak{I}$ is propagated back through the network, these types of networks are widely known as back-propagation neural networks. Once the network is trained, its ability to generalize is validated against a test set of data not used in the training process.

Provided that the training data ere sufficiently representative of the target system being modelled, the network will be able to predict underlying process trends with a high degree of accuracy. Neural networks are essentially data driven, and their performance depends on the quantity and quality of the available data. Their shared and dispersed structure is well suited for use in prototyping and analyzing distributed systems.

If a little time and effort is invested to "dissect" a trained network, one will discover that the internal representation scheme developed by a trained network is not far removed from the method that a detailed system analysis would indicate as the optimal method for controlling a system. If so, the use of neural networks would save quite a bit of time in the early stages of process-control system design. Note that the dynamic nature of training of neural networks opens for modifications of system knowledge whenever a predicted state differs from the actual one.

Software monitoring is a means of controlling the target system. In order to be liable for monitoring, the target system is to be observable as the elementary condition. Preferably, the target system should be controllable[40] as well. The first condition implies that measures can be taken and the state is known at every time, while the second condition assumes the measures to be undertaken on the system are in accordance with the system specifications, input and output.

Control theory presents a range of control algorithms involving feedback, proportional control P, derivative control D (meaning adaptive change of measures) and integral control I (which means registering the history of system change and incorporating the history into the control process). These algorithms are to be embedded into the monitoring software and are henceforth referred to as control software. Control software can operate on various aspects of a target system. Examples include code adaption, convergence control, response time monitoring, adjustment of levels of redundancy, application and modification of measures and the related actions, correctness control, accuracy level, availability, security level control, etc. An outstanding example of the approach of adaptive buffer management in mobile object-based real-time computing using a PID algorithm has been presented in [Ip, Lin, Wong, Dillon, Wang

---

40 Note that observability is a prerequisite for controllability.

2001].

6.5 Monitor correctness

An important issue is to ensure that the monitors themselves are reliable. This is difficult to achieve, as the idea of monitoring the monitors gives rise to an infinite regression of monitors monitoring monitors, without guaranteeing correctness of the top-level controllers. Some unaffected details on performance can however be provided by the monitor itself, without a guarantee of reliability of such reports.

The issue can be dealt with by:
- Maximizing the reliability of the monitoring code by minimizing the complexity of the monitoring code, ensuring the monitors are re-used and are well tested empirically.
- A third party monitoring system in which a third party monitor, known as a monitor coordinator, monitors each of the other process monitors in the the system. Monitor coordinator can be monitored by another monitoring process.
- A system in which there are two independently developed monitors for each process. Both monitors are spawned when a system process is created. The data each monitor reports can be correlated.

6.6 Testing within monitoring environment

If separated from the target application, the monitoring environment can be used to perform tests of both functional and non-functional system requirements. The monitoring environment contains a considerable amount of usage data, which (depending on its volume) is unbiased and representative. This system data can be used to perform system tests by attempting to simulate system failures and automatically find the minimum sequence of inputs required to cause the failure. Under simulations, the user behaviour and system response should, to greatest possible extent, be randomly generated. In the case of monitoring, testing is used both to reveal possible changes within the target system, and to verify changes undertaken by the monitoring environment. Although not recommended, testing can in addition be used for traditional purposes although implemented within the monitoring environment.

6.6.1 Test data generation

A representative amount and type of test data should be generated in the monitoring environment before testing starts. This should be done in a random and unbiased manner. The code for test data generation should be reusable in case there is a need for system migration to a different environment or version upgrade. The same applies to the test application code and test code if any.

It is preferable to generate test data randomly instead of reusing (if any) the existing system data, assumed that the randomly generated test data:
- Is comparable in its data type and size.
- Does not reveal the existing system data contents.
- Does not introduce new features.
- Is generated within the acceptable time limits and using only the assigned resources.
- Can be traced and stored.

The reason for generating test data is the possibility to control data characteristics, preserve security and privacy requirements and prevent any interference with the application which may result in undesired or unpredictable changes on the system being undertaken under testing.

6.6.2 Testing foci

The most common testing technique is regression testing, which is based on the idea that whenever a change has been made on the system, the test is rerun to make sure the desired functionality is achieved.

One can distinguish between a number of different testing foci. The most known ones are:
- The operation test.
- A fault-scale test.
- A performance test.

- An overload test.
- A negative test.
- Requirements based tests.
- Ergonomic tests.
- Testing of the user documentation.
- Acceptance testing. For further details, see [Jacobson 1992].

6.6.3 Levels of testing

Testing can be done at several levels, as illustrated by figure 2.1[41]. *Unit testing* is done at code level. One checks for implementation errors in the program code. This is done with reference to the implementation requirements and standards. The amount of effort spent on unit testing will vary among the components. Fault seeding during unit testing can be done by violating system invariants by passing in out-of-range values or corrupting the data halfway through the procedure. Some of the issues to be checked for include:
- Code effectiveness.
- Priority handling.
- Data (message exchange).
- Memory management.
- Data integrity.
- Clarity.
- Security.

Integration testing is done against the detailed design specifications. In a distributed processor system, each processor is usually unit tested before it undergoes any level of integration. Integration testing adds the components together in a piece-wise fashion. The integration simulates missing or unavailable components as needed. Integration testing checks the interfaces among the interacting components, as well as checking some broad measure of functionality. Fault seeding during integration might be done by:
- Forcing or simulating a component failure.
- Sending messages with incorrect data type.
- Requesting services beyond functionality domain.

---
41 See chapter 2.

System testing is done against high level design specifications. It concerns the entire application. This part is concerned with the end-user aspects of the system. Fault seeding during integration might be done by:
- Making comparisons with the high level design specifications.
- Applying independent test environments which use randomly generated test data.
- Performance measuring.
- Service domain measuring.
- Security breach attempts.
- Integrity level testing.

Acceptance testing is based on system requirements specifications. This test can be performed by formally validating the system requirements statements. The testing is done by the end-user organization. The system is now tested in its real environment. When the test is conducted, the decision can be made whether the system is acceptable or not.

6.6.4 Testing system selections

In certain cases testing can not be performed on the entire system. The alternative is to apply a method already used in a number of projects, where the idea is to select a number of system components, which may represent a certain fraction of the whole system, usually 10 per cent. The components should be selected in such a way that they as a collection form a representative selection containing most of the system features. [Wiger 2001] introduces "10 % component fraction testing, which covers 90 % of service extent".

The method has previously shown to be highly efficient. Assumed that a correct representation of components has been selected, most errors can be revealed under such a testing regime. Test coverage is a commonly used term in this context, which can be defined as the degree to which a test or a set of tests addresses all specified requirements for a given system or component.

A useful tool is the use of statistical methods on the respective components and the entire system. Such an approach will enhance the selection process and keep track of the activities and experiences related to the system.

Operational profile is another method used to keep statistics on the system. It is defined as a set of operations that the software can execute along with the probability with which they will occur. An operation is a group of runs which typically involve similar processing. See [Lyu 1995] for further details.

To determine a usage probability distribution, a number of steps can be undertaken:
- Analyze the system and environments to identify a set of stimuli.
- Apply the stimuli to cause the software to change behaviour.
- Create usage scenarios.
- Assign probability to each stimuli.
- Generate test cases for each stimuli according to the usage probability distribution.

6.6.5 Automation of the testing process

The testing process should be automated to the greatest extent possible. The reasons are many:
- The results will be more comparable between the different tests.
- Errors caused by deviations in the testing method will be eliminated.
- The reusability and reliability of the testing environment will increase.
- Time and resource use will be optimized.

The testing environment should be separated from the target system, if possible embedded into the monitoring environment and consist of:
- The testing documentation.
- Documentation, code and data directories for the different tests named according to the timing of test run.
- Documentation templates.
- Test plans.
- Test result logs.
- Computer aided tools (applications) for statistical analysis.

- Test data.
- Test application system.
- Test code.

The function of a test environment embedded into a monitoring environment will differ from a separated one. Due to performance issues, testing will be undertaken only at certain levels and limited.

The complete process for a separate testing environment is illustrated by a simplified flowchart, as shown by figure 6.4.

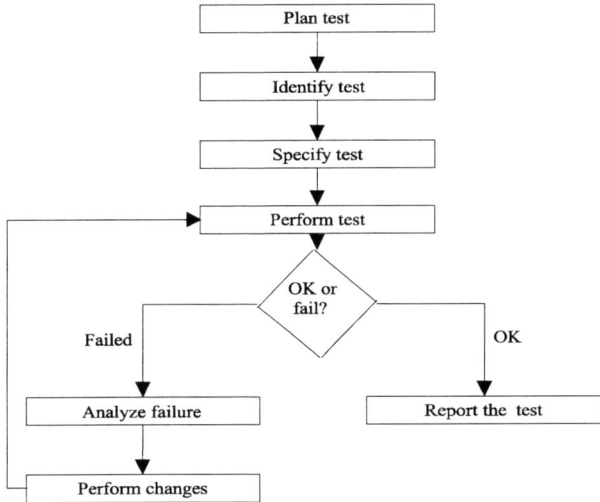

Figure 6.4: Test process stages

Plan test stage includes a number of initial steps, such as:
- State to what degree the test is to be automated.
- Define the objectives on test result accuracy.
- Identify the related standards to be taken into considerations.
- Define the expected degree of reuse.

Identify test stage includes steps such as:
- Estimate the required resources and identify those that are actually available.
- Strive to look for the major failures first.

- Define types of subtests (based on sequence of actions, loops, components, priorities, etc.).

Specify test stage includes steps such as:
- Specify subtests on a functional level.
- Specify how the tests are to be executed.
- Describe the procedure flow.
- Work out documentation standards.
- Identify needed equipment, software and data.

Perform test stage includes steps such as:
- Test data generation which includes mechanisms for seeding random faults.
- Duplication of the target application, its reproduction or selection of component representation.
- Test code execution.
- Logs and reports.
- Result analysis.
- Result approval or failure.

During the result evaluation, a decision table can be used in order to decide whether the test is to be approved or not. A way of doing it can be to multiply importance with the number of failures. As long as the result is below a given threshold the the test is approved and finished.

In case of test failure, the results are to be analyzed in order to find the source of the failure. The most natural questions to be posed are:
- Has the test been performed correctly?
- Are there errors in the test environment?
- Does the test application code/underlying application/component selection behave in accordance with the target application?

These questions should be asked before considering the location/occurrence of a fault in the application. Risk assessment tools can also be used for this purpose.

When the origins of a failure or failures have been identified, changes are to be performed on the system. This should be done so that no new errors are introduced. The changes should be documented and the test performed again. The process is repeated until test approval has been reached.

Note that each stage presented in figure 6.4 can be split up into lower level flowcharts to describe the process entirely. On the lowest levels of the test design system characteristics and design will become important. On the lowest level of test design one will be able to transform the stages into pseudocode/directory structure/data flows/documentation stereotypes/user manuals and so forth and finally implementation. Note that the test environment itself has to be tested to ensure it meets the requirements.

An oracle can be used to evaluate the results of a test. An oracle is, in contrary to the ancient and more common definitions, any (human or mechanical) agent that decides whether the program behaved correctly on a given test. The oracle makes decisions about the test outcome by analyzing the behaviour of the program against its specification. In particular, an input/output (I/O) oracle can only observe the input and output of each test, looking for failures. It is programmed to reject output iff[42] it observes an incorrect output for a given input, and approved otherwise. If the oracle approves the outputs, one can say that the test was successful, otherwise the test has failed.

A more general oracle than the I/O oracle can observe states, the contents of memory locations and registers, in addition to the program input and output, and thus detect a failure earlier.

One must consider that the oracle may not always judge (state validity) correctly. Therefore, the coverage of the oracle should be introduced, defined as the probability that it rejects a test given that it should reject it (including detection of false failures).

Oracle coverage influences system testability, which can be improved by attempts to design for testability. Note that testability is enhanced by increasing the internal observability of the system. This can be achieved by run-time checks and supervision.

---

42 Read "if and only if".

One problem is that programs under test behave differently from the programs in normal operation due to lack of workload, sufficient number and kinds of users, distribution, random triggers, etc. The solution is in either using nonintrusive monitoring or leaving the monitoring software in place during normal operation.

Before the testing is started, one should define the acceptance criteria in terms of either metric expression values or system responses/behaviour for selected scenarios.

Use-cases should be set up and the related acceptance criteria predefined. The tests should be based on the use cases and the triggering events either adjusted to the specifications or randomized.

6.7 Using Erlang as a monitoring programming language

Erlang provides language support such as process creation and communication, concurrency, distribution, dynamic module loading, linking, garbage collection and run-time code update, which enables the development of application and monitoring processes in Erlang itself. Furthermore, Erlang is syntactically simple, which increases development speed. The language has built in mechanisms to handle failures and the libraries contain some limited monitoring support. The high level attributes of Erlang allow the monitoring processes to be written in source language of the development environment.

Erlang supports dynamic runtime loading and unloading of modules, thus the system can be modified and extended while it is still executing. Monitoring processes can then be dynamically linked and replaced at runtime in the same manner as any other module in Erlang. This allows changes to be made in the monitoring software independently of the functional one. Main Erlang characteristics are summarized in appendix B.

6.8 The cost of monitoring

Assessing whether or not continuous monitoring is usable in a real-time system requires careful analysis of the costs of running parallel processes and the performance losses involved.

According to [Graham, Kessler, MsKusick 1983], the intrusion of profiling code can result in up to a 35% slow-down in execution speed of the target application. This is often an unacceptable figure for real-time systems where time constraints are strict.

Further, the intrusion of any extra code into a program, regardless of what the code is, results in a different program even though the functionality may appear to be the same.

The amount of data associated with the monitoring processes is another issue. Operating systems need to support the efficient movement of the data in a way that does not bottleneck the functional processes.

The internal costs of the system, beyond the availability of the multi-processor hardware, include extra memory usage and increase in I/O bandwidth usage.

6.8.1 Monitoring overhead

As with the Heisenberg uncertainty principle[43], any attempt to gain information regarding the execution of a program will interfere with the run-time behaviour of the monitored program because of the monitoring overhead. The causes of the overhead are as follows:
- Increased execution time due to the monitoring code. Resource response time is increased due to increased bus traffic, number of context switches and the number of pipeline stalls.

---

43 "-Measuring program state, perturbs said state.
   -The degree of perturbation is proportional to fraction of the state that is captured, i.e., the greater the volume of information collected, the lower the accuracy." [Lewis, Reed 1988]

- Extra time and space for memory access. The need for extra memory will increase the memory access time by affecting the hit rate, bus skew, propagation delays, data path traffic and I/O waiting states.
- Extra communication. Extra communication will be needed between monitors in addition to the communication between the monitor and target program.
- Extra time for execution of unoptimized instruction code. Owing to the addition of extra monitoring code, certain compiler optimizations may not be applicable to the object code if monitoring object code is added. Therefore, extra time is required to execute the unoptimized object code during the monitoring. In addition, removing the monitoring object code from an instrumented object code will not result in the same object code without monitoring because of compiler optimization.

Communication between the monitor and the target program being monitored is the major monitoring overhead, but it can be reduced dramatically with proper implementation technologies. Two approaches can be used to communicate between the monitor and the target program: shared memory and message passing.

Another issue is the one of synchronization, where either a central or a local timer can be used.

Distributed programs suffer from the so-called probe effect, wherein the execution of monitoring software introduces delays that alter execution, and thereby hide error symptoms. Four methods of minimizing probe effects are:
- To predict the effect of monitoring, and to make necessary adjustments aimed at reducing the interference effect.
- To use hardware devices for data acquisition.
- To separate the monitoring environment from the target system.
- To copy the critical and representative parts[44] of the distributed target system, design communication between the two for purposes of synchronization and consistency and perform all the monitoring activities on the target system copy, but only the actions and modifications on both the target system and its copy.

---

44 These parts can be data, memory, communication and software.

6.9 Run-time monitoring of dependability attributes

To be monitored, dependability attributes should be defined in such a way that they can be collected. This will allow for improvements to be made at each stage of the development cycle and to the general development process because there are concrete measures being continuously collected before each maintenance cycle. These measures allow comparisons between, before and after each system upgrade. The attribute metrics should be system specific, based on requirements and their constraints clearly identified. The metrics should be split into units which can be applied as budgets to internal modules and processes. The sum of budgets should not exceed constraints provided by the user requirements. This allows for determining how to measure requirements for each process.

By having requirement budgets for system components, specific coding targets can be set for individual units of code and larger subsystems. It is these targets that form the basis for unit testing. Finding a mapping between the contract specifications of attributes and the system monitors is the key to providing informative and useful monitors. The use of Erlang simplifies this process, as state is maintained only by a process; not, as in object-oriented systems, by a series of objects each with complex operations that may have side-effects.

The monitoring environment itself will have performance and reliability requirements. Therefore, data volume- and time budgets, based on data flow diagrams and finite state machines, should be deduced on the resource usage within the monitoring environment. With advances in hardware speed and architecture it is possible to have monitoring activities running in parallel with the main software process. Because it is done in parallel, it is done without the intrusive overhead of adding the monitoring code into the target system code as traditional profiling systems do.

6.9.1 Enhancing the process of software development

Monitoring provides useful feedback for different stages of the software development life-cycle. Areas of defects are more efficiently highlighted and improvements can be made throughout the development process. Examples of improvements include:
- Requirements can be traced through development and into operation.
- High level monitoring can monitor the effectiveness of particular design patterns in the system, thus allowing for more effective selection of design units.
- Coding efficiency is improved and corrections made more rapidly.
- Testing is improved by application of statistical usage testing.

6.10 General system monitoring guidelines

As a prerequisite for controlled system monitoring, a number of general guidelines have been summarized:
- Always make sure the dependability attributes that are to be concentrated on during monitoring are clearly defined.
- Instrument the system as it is built to enable measurement and analysis of workload scenarios, resource requirements and performance objectives achievement.
- Define attribute ratings and criteria metrics before starting to work on monitors.
- Utilize any language and hardware advantages when implementing monitors. For instance, monitoring activities can in some cases run in parallel with the main application.
- Distinguish the monitoring environment from the target system environment. Do not allow data and/or processes to interfere with each other and between the two different environments.
- Identify the dominant workload components to allow minimization of their resource consumption and utilize their dominance as representative selection for testing.
- Use monitoring environment to identify the data that are accessed often and duplicate them in order to reduce their retrieval time.
- Generate an error event graph showing the links between the error

generators and error handlers[45].
- Specify which attributes that should be collected for each fault. Examples include:
  - Timing: when did it occur?
  - Symptom: what was observed?
  - Mechanism: how did it occur?
  - Cause: why did it occur?
  - Locality: where did it occur?
  - Consequences: what was the impact of the fault?
  - Repeatability: determine if the fault is an one-time occurrence, intermittent, recurring or reproducible.
  - Severity: to what degree was the user affected?
  - Phase: the life-cycle phase in which the error was encountered.
  - Activity: the activity taking place when the fault occurred.
  - Cost: cost can be expressed in terms of effort, downtime, money etc. This attribute is system specific and can only be evaluated in the context of the other system cost information.
- The monitor should be able to generate the code for data acquisition automatically as requirements and the metric definitions change. Enabling and disabling of acquisition has to be efficient.
- Investigate the faults to obtain their nature and cause and to propose solutions for resolution action or corrective action.
- Maximize the efficiency and minimize the resource usage of the monitoring environment and tune monitors to achieve maximum hardware utilization.
- Keep a log of the monitoring processes and results.
- Automate the monitoring process to highest possible degree, especially for long lasting systems.

The monitoring process can gather information about other working processes and determine which processes should be assigned to which tasks. This can be supported by use of "a load balancing scheme", which functions as a survey of statistical data on past system operation and keeps track of the workload of the different parts of the system. Failure surveying[46] is a similar technique used for keeping track of failures and

---
45 Care needs to be taken when interpreting the collected data because the process that appears to be generating the errors may not be the actual cause of the error sequence.
46 Including historical data on both functional and non - functional system characteristics. Examples include performance, failures and down time.

the ways they can be treated within the system, provided the component interdependencies are given. The monitoring processes should be used as guards in fault-tolerant systems, so that if a fault occurs in a working process the monitoring process evaluates what happened and takes the necessary actions to keep the system in service. This rapid detection reduces overhead associated with fault tracing and repair. If automated, the risk treatment framework from chapter three can be used for this purpose and integrated with the monitors. It is suggested that logging of the statistics of the situations handled by the monitors be conducted with the objective of improving the knowledge of the system, quality of future actions and maintenance.

Supervision is a monitoring technique often used in telecommunications applications implemented in Erlang[47]. A class of behaviour in OTP exists for implementing supervisors. Supervisors handle start, recovery and termination of processes. Structuring the system as a tree is common when using supervisors.

During system testing, it can be difficult to determine if the observed behaviour of a real-time system is consistent with its requirements specification. A system monitor that checks the behaviour against the specification, should be automatically derived from the requirements documentation. The monitor would model the system requirements as a modified finite state automaton in which the states represent equivalence classes of system histories and transitions are labeled with predicates such that it accepts only executions representing acceptable system behaviour.

Logging plays a central role in determining the quality of the system in operation. Systems operation, important events, causes, consequences and statistics need to be logged and stored as persistent data. It is during design, operation and maintenance that logging is most useful.

6.11 Real-time databases in intrusive monitoring

Active or intrusive monitoring approach puts dependability constraints

---

47 See Appendix B.

on a database system containing records on risk analysis and historical experience of the system operation. The data within such a database are constantly retrieved and updated. A database application may also be a part of the target system being monitored. In both cases, similar real-time issues will be raised.

Three types of databases have emerged that encode the notion of time: rollback databases, which record the history of database activities; historical databases, which record the history of the real world; and temporal databases, which incorporate both aspects. The historical database is the most appropriate model of the dynamic state of computation. Historical databases require more sophisticated query languages than conventional databases[48].

Data in real-time databases have to be logically and temporally consistent. The latter arises from the need to preserve the temporal validity of data items that reflect the state of environment that is being controlled by the system. Some of the timing constraints on the transactions that process real-time data come from this need. These constraints, in turn, necessitate time-cognizant transaction processing so that transactions can be processed to meet their deadlines. In addition to the temporal nature of the data, constraints are also imposed on the time taken to respond to a request for it and to use it. Thus, integrity of data in such an application will consist of its correctness, consistency (in case of data replication) and timing requirements on transactions and processing.

Consistency will have two components:
- Absolute consistency - between the actual state being described and the contents of the database.
- Relative consistency - among the data items within the database in case of data replications.

A database will combine several features that facilitate:
- The description of data.
- The maintenance and correctness and integrity of data.
- Efficient access to data.
- The correct executions of query and transaction executions in spite of

---

[48] Temporal QUEry Language Tquel is one that supports historical queries.

concurrency and failures.

The types of transactions can generally be classified into:
- Read only.
- Write only (first creation of the data).
- Update (change of the existing records).

Use of database schemes will help avoid redundancy of data and its description. This is the case in both real-time and non-real-time database applications.
Indexing will assist in efficient access to the data.

Transaction support where transactions have atomicity, consistency, isolation and durability properties, ensures correctness of concurrent transaction executions and ensures data integrity maintenance even in the presence of failures.

In certain cases, timeliness is more important than correctness and a trade-off can be made between the two, particularly when processing time increases with the need to ensure accuracy.

Transactions in real-time databases are of particular importance and the following information can be used in scheduling and concurrency control:
- Deadlines (soft, hard, firm).
- Criticality, measuring how critical it is for the transaction to meet its timing constraints.
- Resource requirements.
- Expected execution time.
- Data requirements.
- Periodicity. Whether the transaction is periodic and the length of the period.
- Time of occurrence of events (read/write requests).
- Properties of the transaction.

Predictability is a central issue for the data integrity of real-time databases. It encompasses both timing and contents predictability. The information above can be used to schedule systems operation.

Overloading is often the main drawback during operation causing the requirements to go unsatisfied.

Lastly, requirements on data accuracy and timing will vary for different kinds of data and at different times. Design should address these issues. For the important achievements in real-time databases, see [Son 1995].

6.12 Further discussion on the benefits of monitoring

Monitoring provides an accurate usage profile of the system. This enables key processes and areas of code to be identified and resources allocated in a cost effective manner to ensure the best perceived outcome for the user. Usage profiles can be applied to all non-functional dependability metrics for appropriate weighting to be given to each component of the system whilst developing plans for statistical usage testing.

Statistical usage testing is a technique that emphasizes efficient use of testing resources. Its philosophy is a user oriented philosophy within which testing for reliability is directed to the areas of the system that receive the most usage.

Transaction budgeting allows the total time for a transaction to be distributed among all the modules which participate in that transaction. This allows a developer to test a module in isolation and to ensure their component is meeting budgeted requirements. Erlang provides granularity from the system perspective as it breaks tasks into multiple cooperating processes. Estimation and measurement can be applied to each process. Monitoring user transactions is done by identifying starting and ending functions for a transaction and monitoring the events generated when these functions are executed. The time difference between the start and end functions, for a particular user, represents the time a user takes to perceive a transaction. An assumption is made that the actual hardware display and users' interpretation of the data is instantaneous.

Other benefits include:

- Improved problem identification.
- Improved stability analysis.
- Continuous verification of dependability attributes.
- Improved performance analysis.
- Improved problem detection.
- Improved requirements traceability.
- Consistent measurements.
- Comparative assessment of several systems.
- Increased granularity, which ensures continuous fulfillment of contracts and allows preventative measures to be taken.
- Iterative process improvement.

Monitoring provides updated information about system stability.

Monitoring provides direct increase of testability of a system. By having a monitor on a process, one essentially has a "tester" collecting results. Including monitors for every process in the system ensures excellent test coverage. It also ensures that the testing is performed throughout the life of the system and that the tests are up to date.

Information concerning long term scalability is also provided by monitoring performance versus load characteristics. Good requirements on scalability are difficult to gather, as changes in most cases are initially unknown.

Results of monitoring can be used to perform inter-system and intra-system comparisons of fulfillment of dependability requirements. Comparisons should be made against systems with equivalent functionality and extent.

By providing improved and updated information about the system, monitoring increases probability of making an accurate risk assessment.

In N-version development, different codes are written for the same application. The same monitor can be used to test all the versions and identify the optimal one.

Executable software contracts for processes within a software system can

be supported within a monitoring process. These contracts are generated directly from initial requirements, should be traceable back to those initial requirements and can be produced by software quality assurance personnel. Executable software contracts can:
- Specify pre and post conditions.
- Specify a series of test cases and results.
- Specify budgets for various measurable software characteristics.

Once compiled the executable software contracts are located within the monitoring code. This has two advantages: requirements are developed and checked independently of the functional modules and user perceived cost of executing these contracts is reduced.

6.13 Maintenance

Failure causes in distributed systems are numerous. Observing what happens in connection with a failure helps at the different facets of maintenance. It will serve as a guideline to describe them. Software maintenance is not caused by wearing out, but by appearance of (previously hidden) defects and changing requirements. What happens before the failure is the subject of preventive maintenance. The aim of maintenance is to minimize failure occurrences. In addition, there are also several ways to detect failures, such as test loops and watch-dogs[49]. Once a failure is detected, a number of immediate automatic measures are taken locally by components directly connected to the component containing the failure. Examples include software reset, taking over the activities in a redundant design or stopping the process. These measures do not prelude repair, and to this avail the failure must be identified (including location) in a precise manner. The actual replacement may involve only the faulty components or imply a modification of all similar modules in the system. The best known ways of minimizing failures are:
- Redundancy.
- Preventative design.
- Test coverage.

---

49 These are independent devices which monitor some aspects of of the activity of a processor or a component.

Regular and automatic monitoring and testing are important fault detection methods. Another source of information which must not be neglected is the feedback from the users themselves. User complaints, one analyzed, often reveal faults that have escaped internal checks.

Several techniques can be used to locate a failure. Different types of alarms may carry sufficient information to identify the fault. In sophisticated implementations, such as expert systems, the analysis may be done with the help of a run-time database where similar faults which have happened in the past can be found. If the first analysis is insufficient, complementary information can be obtained remotely by performing active tests on the system.

Once the failure has been located, a corrective measure can be applied. Corrective maintenance constitutes around 21% of the total maintenance activities. In the case of software errors, correcting the problem requires new, corrected software to be loaded. In the meantime, software patches may be required to reduce the effect of the failure. Alternatively, modifications of the configuration are sometimes used to avoid going through certain routines. Similarly, errors inputted to inconsistencies between cooperating machines/processes can be corrected by changing the configuration.

Preventive maintenance is intended to increase maintainability of the system in future and constitutes around 4% of the total maintenance activities.

The purpose of adaptive maintenance is to let the current system run in changing environment. It covers 25% of the total maintenance activities.

The remaining 50% of maintenance activities are represented by perfective maintenance, which improves the system, adopting it to changed or new requirements.

Monitoring is also used to provide information for perfective and preventive maintenance. This information is fed back into the monitoring environment to ensure predefined actions are taken in future in response of failure conditions being met.

In all cases, a precise location of the fault is of foremost importance to minimize maintenance costs and reduce the time during which service is either degraded or critically sensitive to a second failure.

In the case of distributed systems, although fault detection is mainly a function spread among the traffic handling equipment, a network management system can fulfill a number of useful functions such as alarm centralization, remote testing, alarm or error message analysis to determine the nature of the fault, failure database trend analysis, etc.

An integrated system to support maintenance activities will therefore include central facilities from where the whole network is monitored. Each of the machines or nodes[50] in the network is monitored. Each component/node is linked to one of these facilities. Through these links, alarms can be forwarded and remote tests to localize failures can be commanded.

6.14 Integrity monitoring

Chapter 3 offers a general definition of integrity which can be applied as a starting point in monitoring process. In most cases, however, the definition will be system specific and expressed by only a single attribute-based metric. Further, risk analysis should be performed and risk acceptance level(s)[51] determined. Scenarios should be created, grained and threats (with the related measures) identified. As a result, the following sequence of steps should be followed when developing an integrity monitoring environment:

1. Identify system attributes that characterize integrity.
2. Define ratings.
3. Identify criteria of integrity attributes.
4. Define criteria related metrics.
5. Create scenarios on system and if necessary on component levels.
6. Relate metrics to each system component and make budgets so that the total values do not exceed the budgeted ones.

---

50 Implying both software and hardware.
51 Depending on the number of integrity attributes identified.

7. Define constraints of each component.
8. Monitor the grained metrics on component levels.
9. If a constraint on a component is exceeded, report to the master monitor[52], if any, and log.
10. The master evaluates if the violated constraint exceeds the system requirements when combined with the cooperating components within the scenario.
11. If requirements are violated, report the state and take the necessary actions.

Apart from the output values, the system response on the triggering events should be monitored. This assumes pre-defined scenarios for correct system behaviour, so that the monitoring environment can detect any deviations. Output values can also be included in the scenario. Scenarios can be created at several system design levels, and they should represent requirements. All integrity attributes should be included within scenarios, either separately or in a combination. Metrics should be based on the number of and types of deviations from the scenarios and the corresponding budgets. Budgets can include aspects such as:

- Failures (types, severity).
- Time (data transfer, active time, time between failures, etc.).
- Security measures, breaches.
- Level details.
- Output correctness before action is taken.
- Deviations in behaviour.

System failures and process/component failures should be distinguished and it should be noted that they are not necessarily always related to each other. Attributing a failure to the correct process is often difficult in a concurrent environment. Types of failures related to a single process can vary. Moreover, a single error can cause a cascade of other errors and it is important to identify when the initial error event was generated. An error event graph (a sequence diagram) can be generated, showing the links between error generators and error handlers. When handling error events, careful analysis should be undertaken as processes that appear to be generating the errors still may not be the actual cause of the error

---

[52] A superior monitoring module.

sequence. Familiarity with the system and knowledge systems[53] integrated into the monitoring environment are means of coping with the problem.

One can question what the target application is being compared to under monitoring. Requirements specification, design, risk states and applications release version are but some examples. Scenarios, if used as the basis for monitoring, can be related to any of these on either the system or component levels, or a combination of the two. In best case, each kind of approach should be traceable back to the contract where constraints are clearly defined. Thus, if monitoring environment is based on the design, it should offer a higher level of granularity but also ensure that no errors are introduced under transition from requirements to design.

6.15 Architecture proposal for a monitoring environment

Figure 6.5 illustrates the top level architecture of a monitoring environment derived from the guidelines above. The control sequence within the monitoring environment is as follows:

sense -> process -> compare/analyze -> decide -> act

with a feedback loop from any stage to one or more levels above as appropriate. Identification of the event occurrences is an important parameter which in most cases directly influences the degree of system intrusiveness. The environment is however designed to impose a minimal degree of overhead on the target system and the respective systems[54] do not compete for any resources.

The outcome of the sensing stage is raw data as received through messages, read from the system bus or reported from the sensors. The processing stage delivers a situation report based on the external data. The comparison/analysis stage covers anomalies detection, prediction and analysis of the present state. The decision stage is supported by

---

53 Based on containing results of risk analysis and system history.
54 Monitoring environment, target system and target system copy.

system logic, statistics, intelligence data, risk analysis and dependability requirements. The decisions made are based on knowledge about state, its causes and potential consequences. The outcome are planned actions, updates, modifications and additional testing.

The functionalities the monitoring environment covers include:
- Data acquisition, analysis and processing.
- Filtering.
- Risk analysis and control.
- System data and knowledge databases.
- Testing within a test environment.
- Actions control.
- On-line development tools.
- Human-machine interface (HMI)[55].

Target system is represented by its copy for purpose of simulations, testing and system data acquisition. Actions are always made on the target system copy prior to the intrusion on the target system. In both cases, actions need to be executed atomically, i.e., without being interrupted. To assure their equality, the target system and its copy are frequently compared for the necessary parameters: time, data consistency, volumes, memory, resources etc. The target system is assumed to be sufficiently represented by its copy. As the target system is distributed while its copy is not, the system copy is designed only from the necessary and representative components: CPU, bus, memory, software, performance, data and communication info within the system, etc. To assure consistency between the target system and its copy, program replay can be used. Program replay is a technique for reproducing a particular execution of a distributed program on demand. During the operation, the program is executed and information describing the execution is stored in a log. During a replay phase, the log can be used to guide the execution of the (presumably) equivalent system along the execution part recorded in the log. Equivalence is verified if the same execution path is produced[56]. A drawback of this method is that the

---

55 HMI is a part of the "tools" module.
56 A condition for a reliable result is that the log itself is unbiased and representative in level of detail, volume and type of data. A sufficient log will consist of all the messages received by all processes and the order in which the messages were received.
Another condition is that executions of both systems originate from identical state.

system will have to be taken off operation before performing the replay[57].

All communication between the three units[58] is based on message passing over a communication network rather than by sharing structures stored in common areas in memory. The three units can execute in parallel with respect to each other.

The "tools[59]" module contains the necessary support for program generation and monitoring system maintenance: compilers, data analysis filters, text editors, user interface etc. The tools should allow for on-line program manipulations[60]. A necessary functionality is on-line modification of dependability requirements and risk analysis.

6.15.1 Data acquisition

The system values are, after having been read from the target system copy, buffered and time stamped by the scheduler. The necessary attributes are assigned to the acquired data. Scheduler contains low level rules for interpretation of the bite stream obtained into system states and process recognition. The collected data set represents the variables needed to quantify the pre-defined metrics and ratings[61].

The data interpretation itself is implemented within the "condition monitor" module. Checks and further synthesis of the results obtained is made by the event/state detector module. Event detector ascertains what events of interest to the knowledge base have taken place, if any.

6.15.2 Event recognition

A way of acquiring system data is to record the contents of every message sent or received by processes in the program. The message-passing library can be modified to forward a copy of selected types of messages sent or received into a message log in system data database.

---
57 This to avoid interaction from the environment and additional load.
58 Target system, its copy and the monitoring environment.
59 See figure 6.5.
60 Erlang and VxWorks are examples of such tools.
61 Recall dependability requirements definitions.

The message log and message contents can be examined for undesirable or unexpected communication patterns or for messages containing erroneous values, respectively.

6.15.3 Data processing and system[62] training

System state data are by now ready to be transferred to the "data management" unit which updates the "system data" and "knowledge base" databases and responds to requests for data retrievals. As communication between the two databases and several units is controlled by this module, the scheduling issues need to be addressed. Two types of scheduling may be required to manage the control flow: scheduling of individual units and scheduling of competing processes between each module.

The two databases "knowledge base" and "system data" are logically separated. The data within both databases are at different structured levels. Intelligence from the former database is used to interpret the data from the latter one, perform optimizations and achieve intelligent control. Based on this, the two databases are managed hierarchically.

Data management unit functions as a logical interference mechanism and provides the next module with an advanced interference to enhance the opportunity to abstract the relevant information and optimize queries, thus achieving the needed efficiency. The module[63] also receives system state data from event state detector and test results from the testing unit and updates the two databases. Moreover, the data management unit writes to the knowledge base whenever new system knowledge has been gained either from system database contents, testing current system state or elsewhere. This enables evolution of the underlying logic.

The knowledge base will mainly consist of:
- Dependability requirements.
- Dependability attribute expressions[64] and definitions[65].

---

62 That is, monitoring environment.
63 The data management unit.
64 Quantitative expressions.
65 Qualitative expressions.

- Dependability attribute criteria ant the related metric definitions.
- State rules and adaption algorithms.
- Risk analysis guidelines and procedures.

The system data database will mainly consist of:
- Constants for conversion.
- Testing results.
- Values obtained from measurement and signaling.
- Operational system history and statistics.
- Logs.
- Results of computations, reports of testing, periodical operation and risk analysis.
- Information on system resources and functionalities.

The representation is given in form of an entity-relationship model augmented with the action routines and file indexes. A declarative language should be made available for the specification of the dependencies between the representation of the target system state and the target system requirements. If generalized, action routines can be called from standard libraries. The entity-relationship model has the descriptive power to structure and represent the necessary information about the target system. In managing simultaneous updates and retrievals, real-time database issues can be addressed by designing an embedded communication protocol.

In the training phase the system learns new patterns and this knowledge is later used in the recognition phase. An adequate detail level in the two databases and a structured representation are essential in order to avoid mismatch during pattern recognition. The pattern recognition phase relies on the predefined state machines based on target system characteristics.

6.15.4 Knowledge management

Risk analysis is a further step under the decision making process and handles both pre- and post incident situations. Structuring of system data and logic; filtering, retrieval and possible updates are managed by the data management unit.

The acquired system state data are stored in the appropriate databases and further combined for higher abstraction level interpretation by filtering. Filtering implies selecting only the most interesting events and clustering several events into a single, high level event of interest. Clustering protects from significant losses in information content. In the risk framework, some predictable abstract events of interest are pre-defined. Filtering is also needed for security, where certain processes or users should not have access to particular monitoring information. Filtering may be performed explicitly or implicitly in different places and at various stages. During the design phase of the target system, the event definition language[66] can be used to transform ratings and metrics from the requirements into the related events and variables/message types to be measured. A data manipulation language based on SQL, with some enhancements, can be used to collect primitive and combined events under implementation. Risk analysis can be performed on several abstraction levels, depending on the desired level of monitoring granularity. Ratings and metrics are examples of two such abstraction levels. High level events can be defined in terms of primitive events and the sequencing relations among those events. For reasons that will become apparent later on, it is crucial that event recognition and clustering fulfill timing requirements.

6.15.5 Data analysis

Rules and conditions containing the necessary combination of data and knowledge are sent to the "risk analysis" module by the "data management unit". Risk analysis module identifies potential and current[67] breaches. Because analysis is application specific, it is not considered to be a part of a generalized monitoring service. The process is based on the framework presented in chapter three and the analysis is conducted using a combination of:
- Dependability requirements and metrics.

---

66 EDL, presented in [Bates, Wileden 1982].
67 A problem in this case is that the monitoring environment may mask the presence of an error until long after the original cause unless the state has been pre-specified in the risk analysis or known from earlier system operation. This is why priority is put in breach prediction, rather than recognition after breach occurrence.

- Current system state.
- System statistics. Trend analysis are performed for fault forecasting. This requires correlation of event reports.

6.15.6 System diagnosis and pattern recognition

A report of the risk analysis is sent to the "diagnosis" module. The report contains a listing of possible current system states based on an analysis of the current system info and possible pre-states and causes of the current situation. The diagnosis module assigns the related probabilities and lists up the possible modification alternatives.

In the "fault prediction" module the consequences of the current situation are listed up, and the appropriate criticality levels and probabilities assigned.

6.15.7 Action control and system intervention

This info is sent to the "control module" which acquires the necessary dependability requirements, algorithms, logic, and statistics (trend analysis, historical system data, costs, etc.), if necessary repeats the loop, and based on this, optimizes the actions and sends instructions to the "adaption of system copy" module. As a result, actions are performed on the target system copy. The actions can consist of system/data modifications in form of intervention by executing adaption algorithms, or activation of redundant software/hardware.

Extensibility of the monitoring environment is achieved by separating the tasks related to the different stages of the monitoring process.

*Design Guidelines for a Monitoring Environment Concerning
Distributed Real-Time Systems*

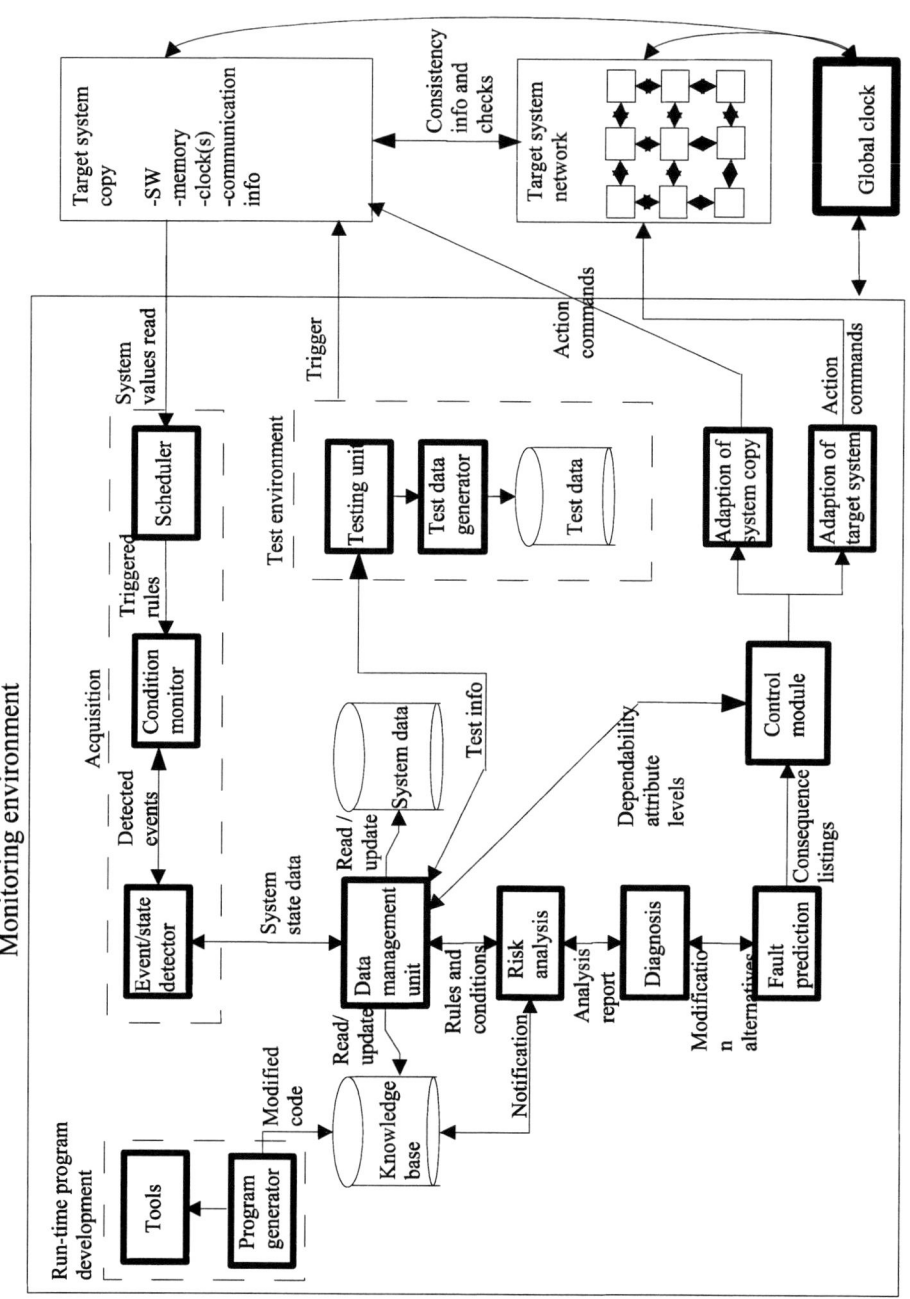

Figure 6.5: Architecture of a monitoring environment

Design Guidelines for a Monitoring Environment Concerning Distributed Real-Time Systems

6.15.8 Action verification

The impact of the actions is verified by the test environment. The test environment helps compensate for the non-determinism of the distributed target system and is used for three purposes:
- Simulation of changes undertaken by:
  - Program generator on either monitoring environment, target system copy or the target system itself.
  - Monitoring environment on target system copy or the target system.
- Verification of changes after an action on the target system copy or the target system has been completed.
- Periodic tests of the system or its parts at the different levels.

Figure 6.6 represents a flowchart for the test environment.

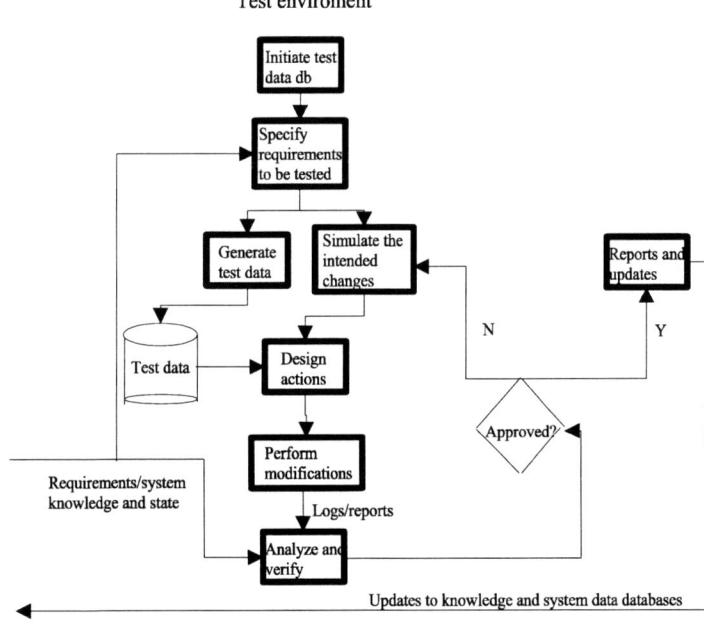

Figure 6.6: Flowchart for the test environment

If the verification[68] has been successful and the desired results obtained,

---
68 Although not required, an extension of risk analysis can include proof algorithms for

the same actions are performed on the target system itself by the "adaption of target system" module. Otherwise, the actions need to be rolled back and the entire monitoring loop repeated. In addition, test environment can be used to simulate actions by triggering appropriate events and to test the system state.

One way of interacting with the target system is by sending new messages or modifying the existing ones.

6.15.9 Implementational issues

Because dynamic adaptions involve making changes to the executing program, it is necessary to maintain consistency of the target system while an action is being enacted. Depending on the type of adaption, it may be necessary for some or all of the components to agree on the instant that the action takes effect.

Dynamic actions must not place an unacceptable overhead on the target system, nor force the program components to wait for long or indefinite periods. The adaption enactments, both successful and unsuccessful, must be processed without major interruptions of the normal flow of the application.

To meet the timing requirements, it may be necessary to introduce redundancy[69] and distribution of the monitoring environment in order to reach the distributed target system more easily. In that case, data acquisition is managed locally by a resident collector, while analysis and control are centralized on a remote monitor.

6.15.10 Simulations and testing

Certain false events can, as indicated above, be triggered to examine the system correctness. Random test data can be generated within test environment for this purpose. The entire test environment is managed by the testing unit, while the test data are generated by the "test data

---
verification of correctness of impact of the actions performed.
69 Meaning software, hardware, communication and data redundancy.

generator" module. The test data are stored in the "test data" database. The test data are generated each time a testing cycle is performed and the database is initialized at start.

An overall test report is sent to the data management unit, which updates the knowledge base and system data databases for the knowledge and report data, respectively, obtained from the testing, see figure 6.5.

6.15.11 Reporting facility

The tailored reports are forwarded to the processing entities needing them. The dissemination can be arranged as shown in figure 6.7. Here the forwarding is based on subscription principle. Processes of a monitoring service can subscribe to a dissemination unit by registering themselves with the subscription service. Each client sends a subscription request indicating their identity, the reports required, and the frequency of delivery. Subscription authorization information, held by the service, is used to determine whether the clients are authorized users and what reports they are permitted to receive. Selection criteria contained within the subscription request are used by the dissemination service to determine which reports and their contents should be sent to the clients. This provides implicit filtering, because only the requested reports are forwarded. The dissemination service is designed within the risk analysis module and the input is the "rules and conditions" data, see figure 6.7.

Design Guidelines for a Monitoring Environment Concerning Distributed Real-Time Systems

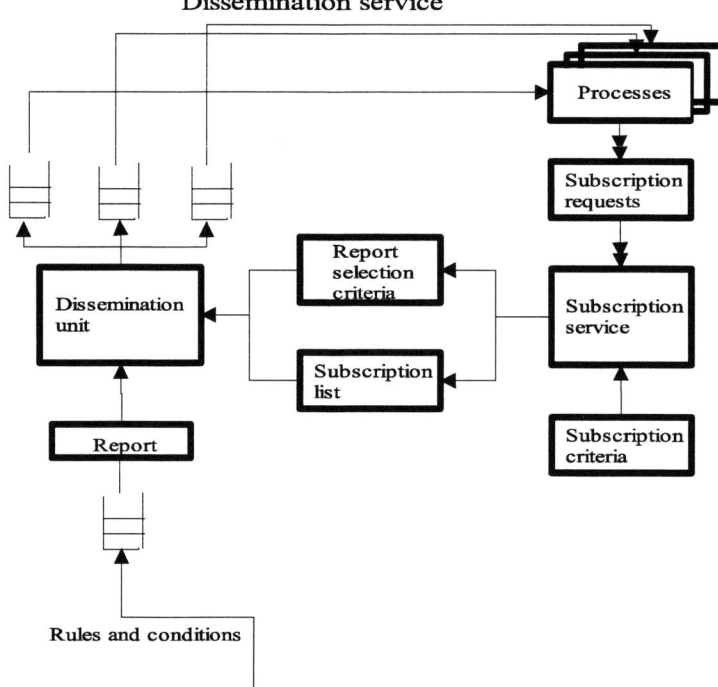

Figure 6.7: Dissemination of reports

The analysis and testing loops are subordinate to the monitoring loop. Each one of them is repeated as appropriate until the desired system dependability level is obtained.

6.15.12 Further implementational issues

Note that data acquired from the target system copy only has meaning when it is associated with time. The greatest difficulty stems from communication delays and unpredictable processing time. There are three main timing issues associated with the architecture:
- Timing consistency within the distributed target system.
- Timing consistency between the distributed target system and the target system copy.
- Timing consistency between the data within the monitoring

environment and the two above.

Messages may be lost, damaged in transit, or delayed for an unbounded amount of time. Although network protocols alleviate the problems of lost or damaged messages, there is no standard mechanism that can guarantee predictable delivery times. Due to the unpredictable delays, it is can be difficult to trace the cause-and-effect relationship between source code and error symptoms in the distributed target program. As a result, a global clock has been introduced[70]. In addition, the observed processes enclose a timestamp with their state messages. This, however, solves only a part of the problem, as target system states may be changed at different times and before the monitoring environment is ready to undertake actions on a previously read state. Thus, in addition to timing consistency, the system is also dependent on state and data consistency which are hard to guarantee unless the monitoring environment offers a timely response[71]. Some kind of data and message redundancy can be introduced[72], as well as state broadcasting. Another condition is regular and frequent data updating. There is also a trade off between timeliness and precision with which the results can be obtained.

The main aspects influencing the response time of the monitoring environment are database response[73], amount of data flow, storage space, scheduling methods used and communication between the modules. Granularity of the readings (as designed from the attribute metrics) will in some cases influence the degree of error due to inconsistencies.

According to [Coulouris, Dollimore, Kindberg 2001], the network performance parameters that affect the speed with which individual messages can be transferred are latency and point-to-point data transfer rate. Thus, the time required for a network to transfer a message

---

70 An alternative is a logical clock which is used to order events according to happened before relation. The principle is that each processor has a local time which is incremented each time response to a timestamped message is received from another processor. This however is not preferred as it requires local instrumentation and would result in additional overhead.
71 Meaning a response within a time period during which the target system state is unlikely to change. Note that unless the response happens on the current (known) state, the monitor acts on an old system state, making action results unpredictable.
72 Note that this will improve performance of a retrieve operation, while an update operation may take longer due to multiple updates within the database.
73 Database response will depend on correctness of updates, database structure and data volume.

containing length bits between two computers is given by:

$$Message\ transmission\ time = Latency + \frac{Length}{Data\ transfer\ rate} \quad [Eq.6.6]$$

The above equation is valid for messages whose length does not exceed a maximum that is determined by the underlying network technology. Longer messages have to be segmented and the transmission time is the sum of the times for the segments.

Within the monitoring environment the crucial parameter will be processor performance.

Another issue is that of variety of hardware, software and data within each one of the systems. The system entities may respond at different times and with different data, thus being incompatible and causing inconsistencies. This can be the case both within the systems (target system, its copy and monitoring environment) and between them. The key has to be standardization.

The data transmission needs to be highly efficient and only introduce message delays within a defined minimum. Deterministic behaviour of the entire architecture, particularly under crisis situations, is important. A condition for this is that only the data needed are acquired at the different times and that these data are maintained where they are actually required. This in turn requires us to know, at a very early stage, what readings are needed and when[74]. Sampling rate which guarantees system observability[75] needs to be determined. This will ensure that a state change between action command sending on the target system copy and verification of desired results based on test results followed by action sending on the target system, will be detected.

When used for the first time on a particular kind of a target system, the system database will not contain data on system history and statistics, while test data can be generated automatically. This will result in more corrective than preventive actions, as the monitoring environment will

---

74 This becomes known once dependability attribute metrics are defined.
75 This should cover both normal and abnormal system operation.

not have sufficient knowledge to predict the undesired state. Some system data may exist though, based on the system state predictions during the risk analysis[76]. If available, statistics should be used in design of the future control systems. In any case, it is recommended to develop the monitoring environment in parallel with development of the target system.

Beyond the scope of this study and due to the automated nature of monitoring environment, is the existence of a visualization service of the monitoring operation, that is a user-machine interface for manual observation and control. If included, it should cover:
- Textual data presentation.
- Time process diagrams. Two-dimensional diagrams require a global or a logical clock.
- Animations.
- Visualization of different abstraction levels.
- Appropriate placement of monitoring information on the screen.
- Use of multiple views.

The major drawbacks of such a service are its complexity and resource exploitation.

In data mining and retrieval some basic functionalities should be provided:
- Pattern discovery. Grouping data records into clusters and then analyzing the similarities of data within a cluster and dissimilarities between clusters allows for reveal of anomalies and identification of new states.
- Trend and deviation analysis using statistics and graphical tools.
- Link and dependency analysis between variables and performance metrics.
- Sequence analysis to model sequential patterns (for example in data with time dependence) to extract report deviations and trends over time.
- Regression for predictive model development.
- Noise filtering.
- Feature extraction to reduce the dimensionality of the signal reduce dependencies between the attributes. Note however that correlations

---

[76] See chapter three.

between the existing variables result in need for fewer variables.

6.15.13 Further implementational issues

To provide continuous monitoring, a dual process model can be taken. Each functional process of interest has a dual monitoring process which is spawned in parallel. This requires minimal program instrumentation, concurrency and message passing support from the operating system. Code intrusion is minimized because each process has its own address space. Some intrusive code, automatically supplied by the compiler, is necessary to ensure that all the monitoring information is passed transparently between the functional and monitoring processes.

Each monitoring process involves some computational and resource overhead. By using a parallel process for the monitoring process, assuming the existence of a highly parallel environment, the perceived performance impact of the monitoring process upon the functional process may be minimized. Ideally the process scheduler in the monitoring environment would be able to schedule both the functional process and the monitoring process at the same time on separate processors. This would provide optimal monitoring performance.

The issue of hardware diversity and number of communication ports can be addressed by using XML [XML] as data description language during message transmission. This will ensure interoperability of the monitoring environment and limit communication overhead.

It is important to ensure that the monitoring process including acquisition, analysis, control, modification, testing and approval can be performed before the state of the target system has changed significantly. If this can not be guaranteed, it is important to design the system so that it stabilizes and delivers readings which will be valid for a necessary period of time[77]. Due to filtering, data volumes will not have significant influence on the response time, provided that retrievals can be done efficiently, for example using views and indexes in the databases.

---

77 This time period is given budgets of monitoring processes.

6.15.14 Timing budgets

Timing is the critical issue for correctness and integrity of the monitoring environment. To guarantee a timely service, one has to ensure that reporting from the target system, reading by the monitoring environment (i.e. data acquisition), processing, analysis and actions, each one representing a separate use case, are performed within given timing limits. Given an exemplar target system, design of a monitoring environment should incorporate deduction of timing budgets based on use cases of the entire network system. The budgets are created by starting with the components or functions that take non-reducible or fast time intervals and carried on by assigning the acceptable timing requirements on the remaining components and functions within the time available for a given use case. As a final step, the design of the remaining components is tailored to reach the assigned timing limits.

Some of the important parameters in the deduction will be:
- Data volumes.
- Processor speed.
- Communication efficiency.
- Implementation techniques.

As a result, the calculations will be highly system dependent.

Another important question is how to ensure the correct (global) state of the target system is known by the monitoring environment at any time and that the state action is performed on is the real state of the target system. Being aware of the correctness of the available state information is in this case more important than just working on as fast response as possible. The problem consists of designing a method or algorithm for guaranteeing that change of a process or a sequence of processes that result in change of the global state will timely be revealed by the monitoring environment when the global state change becomes known.

In addressing this problem, retrieval of prior analysis for each process change will be useless due to timing demands. Instead, pre-designed execution graphs based on use cases should be used. Nodes in the graph can be used to signify significant events in the program's execution and arcs to show the ordering of events or synchronization dependencies between processes.

[Coulouris, Dollimore, Kindberg 2001] presents Marzullo and Neiger's algorithm for deriving assertions about whether a predicate held or may have held in the actual run of a distributed system. The algorithm applies a process collecting states which examines timestamps to extract consistent global states, and it constructs and examines the lattice of all consistent global states. The algorithm ensures observability and is valuable for understanding but involves great computational complexity and is as such only applicable in systems where relatively few events change the global predicate's value.

6.15.15 Performance evaluation environment

Chapter 4.4 considers the issues of parallel performance evaluation. Although it may not be a requirement on the target system itself, performance is an inevitable requirement on the total network. Figure 6.8 shows a general design framework for a parallel performance evaluation environment. Despite being a physical part of the monitoring environment, the performance evaluation part serves as an overall monitor[78] and is as such logically separated from the monitoring environment.

---

78 Meaning that this part monitors not only the target system, but the entire network including the monitoring environment, target system and its copy.

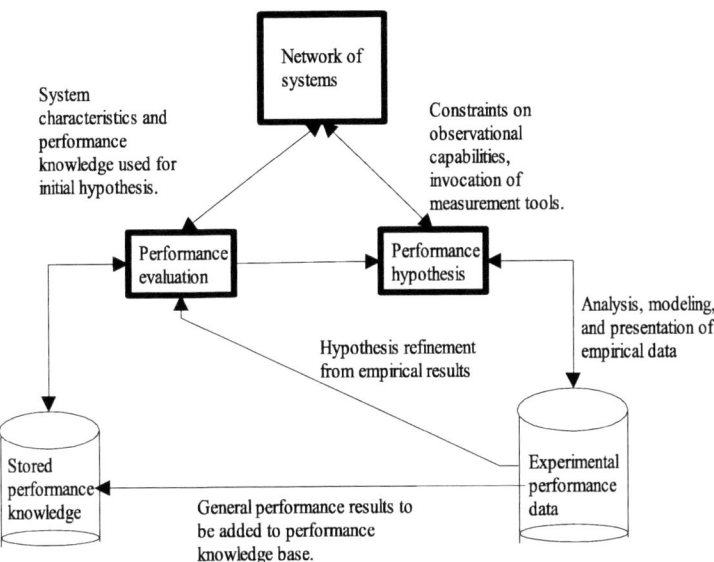

Figure 6.8: General design framework for a parallel performance evaluation environment

The principle is similar to the one of the monitoring environment, but covers the entire network of systems[79] and operates on a higher level where response time is is required to be much shorter and data volume limited. Based on current system characteristics, experimental performance data and earlier knowledge, a performance evaluation is undertaken, resulting in performance hypothesis. The hypothesis are compared with the experimental performance data and database updates made. Due to the change of the performance data, the stored performance knowledge – database is updated. The mechanism is a means for achieving correct and timely response of the monitoring environment to a known and correct target system state.

To achieve controllability one has to combine the advantages of the method above with the timing budgets deduced for the system.

---

[79] Monitoring environment, target system copy and the target system.

6.16 Summary

Software monitoring is a means of controlling the target system. A monitoring facility can dynamically monitor the system and trigger appropriate action if a constraint is violated. Furthermore, it can also be used to test the simulation of the executable specification before the system is operational or even before it is fully implemented.

Redundant software acts as a supervisor by monitoring inputs and outputs of the target system and checking them against the target systems specification.

Run-time monitoring requires the timestamping and recording of relevant event occurrences, analyzing the past history as a computation progresses and providing feedback to the rest of the system.

Monitoring provides an accurate usage profile of the system. This enables key processes and areas of code to be identified and resources allocated in a cost effective manner to ensure the best perceived outcome for the user.

Among the related issues that have been addressed are the ones of control theory, monitor correctness, testing, programming languages, the cost of monitoring, maintenance, integrity monitoring and treatment of dependability attributes.

In case of active monitoring, one will face the issues of distributed real-time databases, which can be addressed in a number of ways.

The approach results in monitoring guidelines and architecture proposal for a monitoring environment.

Chapter 7: Industrial experiences

"There never comes a point where a theory can be said to be true. The most that anyone can claim for any theory is that it has shared the successes of all its rivals and that it has passed at least one test which they have failed."
A.J. Ayer, Philosophy in the Twentieth Century, 1982

7.1 Introduction

Contact with the industry was established with an objective to:
- Reveal the current practices and needs for a monitoring environment for dependability requirements control.
- Get feedback on the applicability of the framework.
- Discuss the ideas and adjust solution to the possibilities and needs.
- Be introduced to the systems and concepts that would benefit from the framework.

7.2 Western Geco

WesternGeco, the world's largest seismic company, provides comprehensive worldwide reservoir imaging, monitoring, and development services, with the most extensive seismic crews and data processing centers in the industry, as well as the world's largest multiclient seismic library. Services range from 3D and time-lapse (4D) seismic surveys to multicomponent surveys for delineating prospects and reservoir management.

A dialog has been established between the author and the company and a presentation of the thesis' main achievements and objectives given. A general introduction to the company's major areas of involvement and main product characteristics has been given by the company, as well as an overall feedback to the presented achievements of the thesis. In addition, an interview was conducted with one of the project managers, see appendix C.

The findings listed up below were revealed during an informal dialog with project engineers and managers. The company works on Seismic Acquisition Systems SAS both on -and offshore. The systems have clear real-time requirements and are geographically distributed (including among others about 40 ships around the world and numerous stations on land). The ships communicate by satellite connections and run continuously.

The company develops parts of SAS and reuse is practiced to a certain degree. The overall architecture of the systems is depicted by figure 7.1.

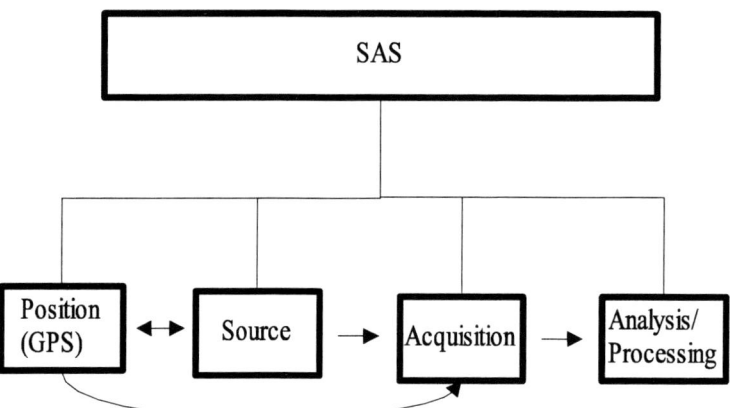

Figure 7.1: Seismic Acquisition System overview

No formal definitions or analysis of the system requirements are deduced at any stage. The opinion is that the framework presented will be relevant in knowledge mining and transfer. A major issue for the company is that substantial knowledge is lost when employees leave. The typical features of the seismic systems are today:
- Must always be available.
- Physical wear is common.
- SW is too complex, it is impossible to design SW well enough and be able to handle failures.
- Performance is a major issue.
- Determinism is highly important.

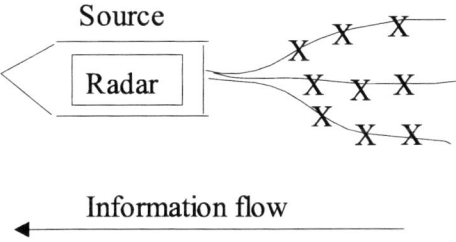

Figure 7.2: A source with cables and sensors

Monitoring[80] is done on component level and embedded into each of the subsystems from figure 7.1. The arrows in figure 7.1 show data flow between the subsystems. The analysis/processing module receives data from all the other three subsystems. The acquisition module uses standard hardware and software. The source in figure 7.2 is a remote object that sends a signal and listens to the response. The sample interval for sensors is 2 ms, while the precision requirement is 10-100 µs (microseconds). Synchronization is a major issue and is managed at a low level.

The experience is that the harder the timing requirements are, the more specialized hardware and software are needed. Specialized components are used at lowest level to achieve timing advantages. It is, for instance, impossible to fulfill 2 ms response requirement using Corba. All the data are time tagged.

The target system is only observed and not controlled automatically. Adaptions of any kind will take at least a couple of seconds and faster corrections are not required. The data that do not meet timing or precision requirements are disregarded or thrown away.

7.2.1 Requirements from the monitoring environment

The monitoring environment would not be expected to perform corrective actions, but to learn and suggest modifications to the operator. There would be a need to update the knowledge base where learning

---

80 In this context meaning data collection.

results and experiences could be retrieved. It might however be the case that corrective actions should be performed on subsystem levels.

The onshore systems are in "critical use", i.e., actively used 30-50 % of total time, while they are running about 100 % of time. The business case does not require 100 % availability of the target systems. In marine industry, however, the availability requirements are 100 %.

The corrective actions are performed manually, and the reason is that:
- Such an approach is feasible.
- Economic constraints are not put on system control.
- This is currently the most reliable way of doing it.

The vision of "One-man instrument room" has not been achieved due to system complexity and amount of work involved in control.

7.2.2 Feedback on the presented monitoring environment architecture

An important benefit from the monitoring environment would be fault prediction and knowledge about MTBF which the current practice does not cover. 50 % of the time, i.e., the fraction when the systems are not running actively, is used to repair failures. It would be useful to collect faults so that they occur simultaneously in order to increase MTBF.

The degree of physical faults and wear of the HW are unsatisfactory and a 10 – doubling of quality of the equipment is needed.

Increasing generalization of techniques is a problem due to a need for extensive reuse. As a result, solutions are not adjusted to the specific requirements and efficiency is, among other attributes, not optimized.

If intended to be developed on an existing target system, a cost-benefit analysis of introduction of the monitoring environment will be needed.

The company has a clear need for a dependability framework encompassing a monitoring environment:
"This will compel us to define exactly what is important, take it through

the development and measure it. It would certainly be of interest to implement the concept with an exception that action module for the target system is substituted with an action recommendation module that would display suggestions to the operator. The test environment should perhaps be excluded as well because of timing requirements and because we do not have a representative enough target system copy and because test of the target system would create intrusion." – **Thorleiv Knutsen.**

The most common requirements the project team or the customer puts on the system are:
- 1 % fault threshold.
- "Good enough".

Two important topics suggested to be discussed in the thesis are:
- What should be done if a target system already has been developed and is in use before applying the dependability framework and introducing monitoring environment.
- What should be done if the functional features of the target system change.

The systems the company is working on already have a module on the top of the hierarchy called Information Manager, which collects numerous randomly selected signals. These are used only for logging and do not have direct collection with the requirements or metrics. The acquisition is based on event push method, i.e., the lower level components message the signals, while it is also possible to ask the system (pull).

"I think there is a business case to implement this. If we had the possibility to build the entire target system from scratch, then we would use the entire concept. Being able to ensure traceability and guarantee requirement traceability is a feature of great value. Another benefit is the knowledge management, which today is completely in possession of employees." – **Thorleiv Knutsen**, referring to the monitoring environment.

7.3 Prediktor

The company delivers software and services for the process industry and is specialized in real-time software for conventional and model-based control, real-time -and relational database technology, software development and web technology, mathematical modeling, model identification, online optimization technology, chemometrics, NIR spectroscopy and instrumentation technology. [Prediktor]

7.3.1 APIS

APIS (Advanced Plant Information System) is a flexible and high performance system for process control, process data logging and presentation of process information on WEB pages. APIS consists of a number of software components. These components can be assembled together to make process supervision or process support systems to optimize plant operation. The components are built with Microsoft COM technology and standard WEB technology.

The products offer streamlined solutions for:
- Easy process data access in real-time for on-line operation, control and optimization.
- Easy access to historical data for reporting, viewing, analysis and model building.
- Web based HMI[81] and reporting solutions.
- Identification of dynamic and steady state process models for use in soft sensing, model based control or optimization.
- Process chemometrics focused on use in online applications.
- Conventional analog and logic control. For a detailed system presentation, see [Prediktor].

7.3.2 Feedback on the presented monitoring environment

Espen Krogh, the contact person in the company was presented the headlines of the concept and questioned about the role of the alarm

---
81 Human-machine interface.

system within APIS.

"When it comes to the alarm system, it has a very simple functionality in our system. We only have what is necessary to monitor simple low level alarms, discrete alarms and quality of the signal. Except from simple checks of values and their qualities, no additional intelligence is used in I/O connected to APIS.

Introducing a concept similar to what you have would deserve a separate processing module with the same structural position in APIS as the alarm module. That would need to be implemented from scratch." -**Espen Krogh, Prediktor**

7.4 Department of Computer and Information Science, Intelligent Systems Group

An informal interview with scholar Pavel Petrovic, doctoral student and member of artificial intelligence group at Department of Computer and Information Science, NTNU [IDI, AI] has been conducted. The purpose was to present the developed framework and reveal useful methods and techniques for efficient knowledge handling. Pavel's thesis project is about evolving controllers for Behavior-Based robots using Incremental Evolution.

Among the discussed topics were case-based reasoning, expert systems knowledge representation, programming languages, neural networks and optimization techniques.

The group is working on a number of projects related to case-based reasoning and the methods are applied on several types of systems. Case-based reasoning is:
- A problem solving paradigm and a machine learning technique within Artificial Intelligence.
- Utilizes the specific knowledge of previously experienced, concrete problem situations (cases).
- A new problem is solved by finding a similar past case, and reusing it in the new problem situation.

- An approach to incremental, sustained learning, by retaining new experiences for future problems.

The method is depicted in figure 7.3 below.

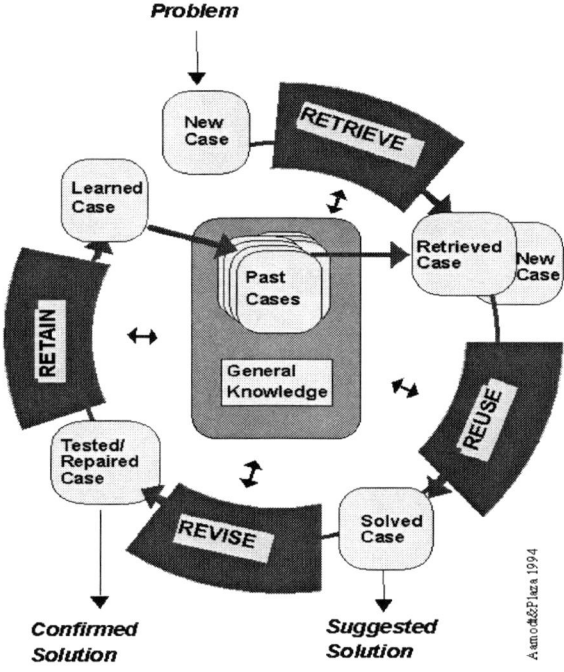

Figure 7.3: Case-based reasoning

A drawback with the method is that undefined states and actions are impossible to handle automatically, as well as extensive data volumes which result in increased processing time. The method is therefore hardly applicable in for example robotics or other real-time systems. This is the so-called symbolic approach to the artificial intelligence where attributes are defined and described to a certain level of detail.

The efficiency related problems are solved by using subsymbolic representation implemented in neural networks. This is a low-level numerical approach which involves few abstraction levels and is extremely fast, although not completely reliable.

Knowledge representation and retrieval is most efficiently done using logical approach, described by, for example, Prolog programming language while message passing could be handled by QNX.

Other techniques for efficient retrieval and optimization are generic algorithms and Simulated Annealing through Tabu Search where the search is first performed on a set of cases and then one or a small group of cases is examined, modified and handled.

7.5 Summary

The contacts that have been established, including a varied representation of industry and academia, have varied in feedback, role and usefulness. The comments received have confirmed originality and applicability of the results, as well as given valuable suggestions on possible modifications and extensions.

The established contacts have also contributed to the adjustment of the study to the existing industrial needs and technologies available.

Chapter 8: Conclusions and further recommendations

*"On its best-behaved day,
the world is still only piece-wise linear."*
Book of Douglass, Law 75

8.1 Conclusions

The dependability framework gives the main general guidelines on dependability specification, implementation, measurement and assessment. It represents a new, quantified, integrated and generally applicable approach. The developed metrics are relevant for both requirements specification and measurement during monitoring. Dependability attributes are hard to discuss in general terms. The fact that they are highly system dependent demands numerous aspects to be taken into consideration and places clear constraints on the possibility to generalize.

The integrity approach is also very general and only certain aspects of it will be likely to be applied on various systems. Important contributions have been made in defining and relating integrity to dependability and risk by means of risk levels.

The notion of risk, strongly tied to the rest of the work, has been given detailed treatment. Framework for risk analysis, integrated with a dependability and monitoring approach, has been developed.

The main issues of real-time and distributed that are related to the monitoring environment part of the study, have been addressed and discussed in detail.

The monitoring approach takes advantage of the results from the dependability, integrity, risk analysis and real-time distributed systems and integrates them into the active monitoring method as a collected means of incremental dependability enhancement during system operation.

Among the overall aspects related to this study, considered, as needed, throughout the work and in connection with the major topics, have been real-time issues, distributed systems, maintainability, total quality management and user requirements.

Dependability can only be achieved by continuous supervision during the entire project life-cycle and by the involvement of all the stakeholders. Dependability requirements should be specified, measurable, instrumented into the design process, tested, monitored, observable and controllable. System characteristics will demand some special aspects to be considered in the process and suggest relevant techniques. The study recommends approaches during the main system life-cycle stages and provides guidelines for these. The process should take the theoretical guidelines into account, as well as benefiting from earlier project experiences. Further, the choice of development tools and technology appears to be one of the decisive factors in implementation.

The main results include design guidelines and architecture proposal for a monitoring environment, taking into account all the previously discussed topics. An informal verification of the usefulness and originality of the results obtained was made through contact with representative parts of the industry.

8.2 Recommendations

Recommendations for further research in the area include as the most relevant matters:
- Develop the remaining metrics related to the identified dependability-attribute criteria.
- Implement a prototype of a monitor for an exemplar system to examine utility of the integrated active-monitoring approach.
- Include hardware aspects in more detail.
- Extend design guidelines of the monitoring environment to encompass documentation and reporting techniques and the related directory structures which would support manual change management.

- Design a CASE tool for risk-analysis framework application and a knowledge-base system that will be applicable as a part of the monitoring framework.
- Relate the study to an economic approach. For example, [Boehm 1981] treats most of the relevant topics in detail and would be an excellent starting point.
- Develop software methodologies and the related libraries containing implemented solutions[82] to the identified risks.

This study represents only a limited contribution toward solving the difficult issue of dependability assurance and control. Future studies can generally go in two directions:
- A detailed approach into monitoring during operation, or
- Development of guidelines for handling dependability requirements related to the remaining two areas: revision and transition.

---

[82] That is, algorithms for monitor intervention aimed at reparation and modification of (parts of) the target system.

Bibliography

[Aredo 1998] Aredo, Demissie Bediye, *Monitoring and Visualization of Distributed Systems*, Department of Informatics, University of Bergen, Norway, January 1998

[Armstrong, Virdin, Wikstrom, Williams] Armstrong, Joe, Virdin, Robert, Wikstrom, Claes, Williams, Mike, *Concurrent programming in Erlang*, Second Edition, Ericsson Telecommunication Systems Laboratories Prentice Hall

[Armstrong 1996] Armstrong, Joe, Erlang - *A survey of the language and its industrial applications*, Computer Science Laboratory, Ericsson Telecommunication Systems Laboratory, September 1996

[Arthur 1993] Arthur, Lowell Jay, *Improving Software Quality, An Insider's Guide to TQM*, Wiley Series In Software Engineering Practice, 1993

[Barbacci 1995] Barbacci, Mario; Klein Mark; Longstaff, Thomas H. & Weinstock, Charles B., *Quality attributes (CMU/SEI-95-TR-021)*. Pittsburg, PA: Software Engineering Institute, Carnegie Mellon University, 1995

[Basili 1992] Basili, V. *Software Modeling and Measurement: the Goal/Question/Metric Paradigm*, University of Maryland Computer science Technical Report, CS-TR-2956, September 1992

[Basili and co-workers 1986] Basili, V., Selbi, R. & Jutchnes, D., *Experimentation in Software Engineering*, IEEE Transactions on software engineering SE-12(7) July 1986

[Bates, Wileden 1982] Bates, P., Wileden, J. C., "*EDL: A Basis for Distributed System Debugging Tools*" Proceedings of 15th Hawaii International Conference on System Sciences, January 1982, pp. 86-93

[Bertolino, Strigini 1996] Bertolino, Antonio, Strigini, Lorenzo, *On the*

Use of Testability Measures for Dependability Assessment, IEEE Transactions on Software Engineering, Vol 22, no 2, February 1996

[Blazevicz, Ecker, Plateau, Trystram 2000] Blazevicz, Prof. Dr. Jacek, Ecker, Prof. Klaus, Plateau, Prof. Brigitte, Trystram, Prof. Denis, *Handbook on Parallel and Distributed Processing*, Springer 2000

[Blesa, Zambardino 1990] Blesa P., Zambardino, R., *Incidence of Parameters in the performance of a Distributed Database*, Workshop Series 1990, Number 6

[Boehm 1981] Boehm, B. W., *Software Engineering Economics*, Prentice Hall, Inc, Englewood Cliffs, New Jersey 07632, 1981

[Bowen 1985] Bowen, T. and co-workers, *Specification of Software Quality Attributes*, 3 vol. RADC Report TR-85-37, February, 1985

[Butcher 1983] Butcher, D.W, *On-line Monitoring of Continuous Process Plants*, Ellis Horwood Limited, 1983

[Carlsson, Gustafson 1998] Carlsson, Anna-Karin, Gustafson, Fredrik, Quality of Telecommunications Applications Software, M. Sc. thesis conducted at SERC, RMIT University Melbourne, September 1998

[Castro 1998] Castro, Maurice, *Erlang in Real Time*, notes for "CS584 Real Time and Concurrent Systems" at RMIT University

[Castro 2000] Castro, Maurice, *Magnus Interface Hardware*, Software Engineering Research Centre, RMIT University, Melbourne. August 3, 2000

[Castro 2001] Castro, Maurice, *The EC Erlang Compiler*, Software Engineering Research Centre, RMIT University, Melbourne, 2001

[Coulouris, Dollimore, Kindberg 2001] Coulouris, George, Dollimore, Jean, Kindberg, Tim, *Distributed Systems Concepts and Design*, Third Edition, Addison-Wesley 2001

[Douglass 1999] Douglass, Bruce Powel, Doing Hard Time; *Developing Real-Time Systems with UML, Objects, Frameworks and Patterns*, Rational Software Corporation, 1999

[Dovich 1990] Dovich, Robert A., *Reliability Statistics*, ASQC Quality Press 1990

[Evans, Marciniak 1987] Evans, Michael W., Marciniak, John J., *Software Quality Assurance and Management*, A Willey-Interscience Publication, 1987

[Feigenbaum 1983] Feigenbaum, A.V., *Total Quality Control, 3rd Edition*, McGraw-Hill Book Co., Inc., New York, 1983

[Filho, 1999] Filho, Antonio Mendes da Silva, *Toward More Reliable Telecom Syetems*, Department of Informatics, State University of Maringa, IEEE 1999

[Fraser, Vaishnavi 1997] Fraser, Martin D., Vaishnavi, Vijay K., *A Formal Specifications Maturity Model*, Communications of the ACM, December 1997/Vol. 40, No. 12

[Glos 1993] *IEEE Standard Glossary of Software Engineering Technology, Australian standard*, AS 3611-1993, IEEE 1993

[Goodman 1992]Goodman, Paul, *Practical Implemantation of Software Metrics*, McGrow-Hill Book Company, 1992

[Graham, Kessler, MsKusick 1983] Graham, S., Kessler, P, MsKusick, M., gprof: *A Call Graph Execution Profiler*. Technical Report, University of California, 1983

[Hansson, Soederberg 2001] Hansson, Peter and Soederberg, Madeleine, *Design Guidelines for Telecommunication Systems Implemented in Erlang*, a M. Sc. thesis conducted at SERC, RMIT University Melbourne, September 2001

[Howden, Huang 1994] Howden, William E., Huang, Yudong, *Software*

Trustability, CSE, UCSD, La Jolla, CA, IEEE Article 1994

[IEEE 1985] IEEE, *Fault Tolerant Computing,* The Fifteenth Annual International Symposium on Fault-Tolerant Computing, IEEE Computer Society, 1985

[Ip, Lin, Wong, Dillon, Wang 2001] Ip, May T. W.; Lin, Wilfred W. K.; Wong, Allan k. Y.; Dillon, Tharam S.; Wang Dianhui, *An Adaptive Management Algorithm for Enhancing Dependability and Performance in Mobile-Object-Based Real-time Computing*, Department of Computing, Hong Kong Polytechnic University, Hungham, Kolwoon, Hong Kong SAR P.R.China, IEEE 2001

[Isaksson, Sturesson 1999] Isaksson, Johanna, Sturesson, Elinor, *Design Guidelines for Erlang*, M. Sc. thesis conducted at SERC, RMIT University Melbourne, September 1999

[ISO8402 1986] ISO 8402-1986, *Quality - Vocabulary,* ISO, 1986

[Jacobson 1992] Jacobson *Object-Oriented Software Engineering,* Adisson Wesley 1992

[Joyce, Lomow, Slind, Unger 1987] Joyce, J., Lomow, G., Slind, K., Unger, B., M*onitoring Distributed Systems,* ACM Transactions on Computer Systems, Vol. 5, No. 2, May 1987, pp. 121-150

[Kan 1995] Kan, Stephen H., *Metrics and Models in Software Quality Engineering*, Addison-Wes;ey Publishing Company, 1995

[Kiang 1995] Kiang, David, *Harmonization of International Software Standards on Integrity and Dependability,* Bell-Northern Research, Ontario, Canada 1995

[King, Schrems 1978] King, John Leslie, Schrems, Edward L., *Cost-Benefit Analysis in Information Systems Development and Operation,* The URBIS Group, Public Policy Research Organization, University of California, Irvine, Califirnia, Computing Surveys, Vol. 10, No. 1, March 1978

[Knuth, Rodd 1990] Knuth, E., Rodd, M. G., *Distributed Databases in Real.Time Control,* Workshop Series 1990, Number 6

[Kramer 1994] Kramer, Jeff, *Distributed Software Engineering,* Invited State-of-the-Art Report, Department of Computing, Imperial College, London, SW& 2BZ, IEEE 1994

[Krishna 1997] Krishna, C.M., Shin, Kang G. *Real-Time Systems,* WCB McGraw-Hill 1997

[Lewis, Reed 1988] Lewis, Paul C., Reed, Daniel A, *Debugging Shared Memory Parallel Programs,* ACM SIGPLAN and SIGOPOS Workshop on Parallel and Distributed Debugging, May 1988, pp. 322-324

[Lyu 1995] Lyu, Michael R. *Handbook of Software Reliability Engineering,* IEEE Computer Society Press 1995

[Manber 1989] Manber, U., *Introduction to Algorithms: A Creative Approach,* Addison-Wesley, 1989

[Marciniak, 1994] Marciniak, John J., *Encyclopedia of Software Engineering,* 2 volumes, A Wiley-Interscience Publication John Wiley & Sons, Inc, 1994

[Marcus, Stern 2000] Marcus, Evan, Stern, Hal, *Blueprints for High Availability,* Wiley 2000

[McCall 1977] McCall, J., Richards, P. & Waters, G. *Factors in software quality,* 3 vol. NTIS AD-A049-015, 015, 055, November 1977

[Mouly, Pautet 1992] Mouly, Michael, Pautet, Marie-Bernadette, *The GSM System for Mobile Communication,* ISBN 2-9507190-0-7, 1992

[Mullender, 1993] Mullender, Sape, *Distributed Systems, 2nd edition,* Addison-Wesley Pub. Co. 1993.

[Musa 1998] Musa, John, *Software Reliability Engineering.* McGraw-

Hill, 1998

[Nato 1984] NATO AQAP-1: NATO *Requirements for an Industrial Quality Control system*, NATO, 1984

[Neumann 1995] Neumann, Peter G., *Computer Related Risks*, Addison-Wesley 1995

[Nissanke 1997] Nissanke, Nimal, *Realtime Systems* University reading, Prentice Hall Series in Computer Science 1997

[Oakland 1989] Oakland, J.S., *Total Quality management*, Heinemann Professional Publishing, Oxford, UK 1989

[Omerovic 2001] Omerovic, Aida, *An Integrated Approach to Dependability of Real-Time Telecommunications Applications Systems*, a project thesis conducted at SERC, RMIT University Melbourne, November 2001

[O'Brien 2000a] O'Brien, Prof. Fergus, *Magnus Applications - Top Ten*, Software Engineering Research Centre, RMIT University, Melhourne, May 2000

[O'Brien 2000b] O'Brien, Prof. Fergus, *White Paper - Magnus Overview*, Version 3.0, Software Engineering Research Centre, RMIT University, Melhourne, September 2000

[O'Brien 2000c] O'Brien, Prof. Fergus, *White Paper - Magnus Applications*, Version 1.0, Software Engineering Research Centre, RMIT University, Melbourne, September 2000

[O'Brien 2000d] O'Brien, Prof. Fergus, *Psion Project (PDA)*, Software Engineering Research Centre, RMIT University, Melbourne, January 2000

[O'Brien 2000e] O'Brien, Prof. Fergus, *CS474 Software Architectures, course material*, RMIT University Melbourne 2000

[O'Brien 2000f] O'Brien, Prof. Fergus, *The Magnus Family of Systems, Product Description*, Software Engineering Research Centre, RMIT University, Melbourne, September 2001

[Paton, Diaz 1999] Paton, Norman W., Diaz, Oscar, *Active Database Systems*, ACM Computing Surveys, Vol. 31, No. 1 March 1999

[Peng, Wallace 1993] Peng, Wendy W., Wallace, Dolores R., *Software Error Analysis*, Computer Systems Technology US Department of Commerce, National Institute of Standards and Technology 1993

[Persson, Nilsson 1999] Persson, Kristian, Nilsson, Marcus, *Executable Contracts, A Lightweight CORBA Approach to Periodically Used Software*, M. Sc. thesis conducted at SERC, RMIT University Melbourne, September 2001

[Pfleeger and Fitzgerald 1991] Pfleeger, S.L., Fitzgerald, J.C., *Software Metrics Tool Kit: Support for Selection, Collection and Analysis*, Information and software technology, Sept 1991

[Pham 1992] Pham, *Fault-Tolerant Software Systems, Techniques and Applications*, IEEE Computer Society Press & The Institute of Electrical and Electronics Engineers 1992

[Powell 1994] Powell, David, *Distributed Fault Tolerance: Lessons from Delta-4*, IEEE Micro February 1994

[Pressman 2001] Pressman, Roger S., *Software Engineering, A Practitioner's Approach*, McGraw-Hill Higher Education 2001

[Randell 1998] Randell , B., *Dependability - A Unifying Concept*, Department of Computing Science, University of Newcastle upon Tyne, IEEE Technical Report 1998

[Randell 2001] Randell, Robert, *A Business Card Server*, Software Engineering Research Centre, RMIT University, Melbourne, SERC-XXXX June 2001 Issue 1, a Technical Report

[Reilly 1990] Reilly, Matthew H., *A Performance Monitor for Parallel Programs*, Academic Press INC, 1990

[Robertson 1996] Robertson, Suzanne, *An Early Start to Testing: How to Test Requirements*, A paper presented at EuroSTAR '96, Amsterdam, December 2-6, 1996

[Rook 1990] Rook, Paul, *Software Reliability Handbook*, Centre for Software Reliability, City University, London, UK, Elsevier Applied Science 1990

[Schulmeyer, McManus 1998] Schulmeyer, G.Gordon, McManus, James I., *Handbook of Software Quality Assurance, 3rd Edition*, Prentice Hall. 1998

[Shneiderman 1998] Shneiderman, Ben, *Designing the User Interface, strategies for Effective Human-Computer Interaction, 3rd Edition*, Addison Wesley Longman, 1998

[Shaw 2001] Shaw, Alan, C., *Real-Time Systems and Software, 1. Edition*, John Wiley 2001, pp 1-49

[Siewiorek 1992] Siewiorek, Daniel P.& Swarz, Robert S., *Reliable Computer Systems 2.nd ed*. Digital Equipment Corp. 1992 ISBN 1-55558-075-0

[Sivertsen, Groven 1998] Sivertsen, Ronny B. And Groven, Kjetil, *net.Monitor*, Høyskolen i Molde, spring 1998

[Six Sigma 2001] Financial Review 24. October 2001

[Snodgrass 1988] Snodgrass, Richard, *A Relational Approach to Monitoring Complex Systems*, University of North Carolina, ACM Transactions on Computer Systems, Vol. 6, No. 2, May 1988, pp. 157-196

[Somerville 1997] Sommerville, Ian, *Software Engineering*, Lancaster University, Fifth Edition, Addison-Wesley, 1997

[Son 1995] Son, Sang, H., *Advances in Real-Time Systems*, Prectice Hall, 1995

[Skapura 1996] Skapura, David M., *Building Neural Networks*, Addison-Wesley Publishing Company 1996

[Stankovic 1996] Stankovic, John A. et al., *Strategic Directions in Real-Time Embedded Systems*, department of computer Science, University of Virginia, Charlottensville, VA 22903, ACM Computing Surveys, Vol. 28, No. 4, December 1996

[Suri, Walter, Hugue 1995] Suri, N., Walter, C. J., Hugue, M. M., *Advances i Ultra-Dependable distributed Systems*, IEEE Computer Society Press, 1995

[Torstendahl, 1997] Torstendahl, Seved, *Open Telecom Platform*, Ericsson Review No 1, 1997

[Tsai, Yang 1995] Tsai, Jeffrey J.P., Yang, Steve J. H. *Monitoring and Debugging of Distributed Real-Time Systems*, IEEE Computer Society Press, 1995

[Tsai, Bi, Yang, Smith 1996] Tsai, Jeffrey J.P., Bi, Yaodong, Yang, Steve J.H., Smith, Ross A. W., *Distributed Real-Time Systems – Monitoring, Visualization, Debugging, and Analysis*, A Wiley & Sons INC, 1996

[Tseng, Fogg 1999] Tseng, shawn, Fogg, B. J., *Credibility and Computing Technology*, Communications of the ACM, May 1999/Vol. 42, No. 5

[Vidyasagar 1997] Vidyasagar, M., *A Theory of Learning and Generalization With applications to Neural Networks and Control Systems*, Springer 1997

[Wallace, Kuhn, Cherniavski 1991] Wallace, Dolores R., Kuhn, D. Richard, Cherniavski, John C., *Proceedings of the Workshop on High*

Integrity Software; Gaithersburg, MD January 22-23, 1991. Computer Systems Technology US Department of Commerce, National Instittute of Standards and Technology 1991

[Wallace, Ippolito, Kuhn 1992] Wallace, Dolores, R., Ippolito, Laura M., Kuhn, D. Richard, *High Integrity Software Standards and Guidelines*, Computer Systems Technology US Department of Commerce, National Instittute of Standards and Technology 1992

[Wallace, Ippolito, Kuhn 1994] Wallace, Dolores, R., Ippolito, Laura M., *A Framework for the Development and Assurance of High Integrity Software*, Computer Systems Technology US Department of Commerce, National Instittute of Standards and Technology, December 1994

[Wiger 2001] Wiger, Ulf, *Four-fold Increase in Productivity and Quality, Industrial Strength Functional Programming in Telecom-Class Products*, FemSYS 2001 Deployment on distributed Architectures, Revision C, Ericsson 2001

[Wong 2001] Wong, Geoff, *Continuous Systems Monitoring*, Department of Computer Science RMIT University, August 2001

[Wong 2001b] Wong, Geoff, *Performance and Reliability Monitoring*, Software Engineering Research Centre, RMIT University, 2001

WWW sources:

[Computer science dictionary] http://hpcn.dsi.unifi.it/~dictionary/

[Erlang] http://www.erlang.se/

[European Dependability Initiative]
http://www.cordis.lu/esprit/src/stdepend.htm

[IDI, AI] http://www.idi.ntnu.no/grupper/ai/

[Papers on dependability] http://citeseer.nj.nec.com/434860.html

[Petri Nets] http://pdv.cs.tu-berlin.de/~azi/petri.html

[Prediktor] http://www.prediktor.no

[XML] http://www.xml.com

Appendix A: Elementary definitions

Active replication: a technique in which all replica managers process all requests independently.

CASE (Computer Aided Software Engineering) tools: software tools that assist with software design, requirements traceability, code generation, testing and other software engineering activities.

Data transfer rate: the speed at which data can be transferred between two computers in the network once transmission has begun, usually quoted in bits per second. [Coulouris, Dollimore, Kindberg 2001]

DBMS: database management system. A system operating on a database application which can be managed and evolve.

Firm real-time requirements: the kind of timing requirements where individual deadlines may be missed, as long as two things occur. First, a sufficient average performance at all times. Second, each deadline must be met no later than at a certain time. [Douglass 1999]

Hard real-time systems: systems that, without exception, must meet their timing constraints - if a constraint is violated, the system fails. [Shaw 2001]

Hazard: an activity, arrangement, circumstance, event, occurrence, phenomenon, process, situation, or substance that is an actual or potential cause or source of harm; a condition that may lead to a mishap.

High integrity software: software that must and can be trusted to work dependably in some critical function, and whose failure to do so may have catastrophic results, such as serious injury, loss of life or property, business failure or breach of security.

Integral control (I): registering the history of a system or a components behavioural aspect and incorporating the history into the control process.

Latency: the delay that occurs after a send operation is executed before data starts to become available at the destination. [Coulouris, Dollimore, Kindberg 2001]

Metric: the definition, algorithm or mathematical structure used to make a quantitative assessment of product or process.

Middleware: the term middleware applies to a software layer that provides a programming abstraction as well as masking the heterogenity of the underlying networks, hardware, operating systems and programming languages. CORBA is an example. Some middleware, such as Java RMI supports only a single programming language. All the middleware deals with the differences in operating systems and hardware. In addition to solving the problems of heterogenity, middleware provides a uniform computational model for use by the programmers of servers and distributed applications. Possible models include remote object invocation, remote event notification, remote SQL access and distributed transaction processing. For example, CORBA provides remote object invocation, which allows an object in a program running on one computer to invoke a method of an object in a program running on another computer. Its implementation hides the fact that messages are passed over a network in order to send the invocation request and its reply.

Mishap: an unintended event that causes an undesirable outcome.

Mobile code: the term mobile code is used to refer to code that can be sent from one computer to another and run at the destination. Since the instruction set of a computer depends on its hardware, machine code suitable for running on one type of computer hardware is not suitable for running on another. The virtual machine approach provides a way of making code executable on any hardware: the compiler for a particular language generates code for a virtual machine instead of a particular hardware order code for the Java virtual machine, which needs to be implemented once for each type of hardware to enable Java programs to run.

Passive replication: a technique in which fault tolerance is achieved by directing all requests through a distinguished replica manager and having a backup replica manager take over if this fails.

Primitive measure: a measure obtained by direct observation, often through a simple count.

Primitive metric: a metric whose value is directly measurable or countable.

Process: any specific combination of machines, tools, methods, materials and/or people employed to attain specific qualities in a product or service.

Profiler: a tool which monitors the time the CPU spends executing individual routines within a system and counts the number of times functions are executed. Profilers report how execution activity is distributed over the body of the code. While normally considered performance tuning tools, profilers that count each instruction execution (as opposed to sampling them) can be used to report loop iterations and other execution patterns.

Redundancy: the presence of backup components that perform the same or similar functions as other components.

Response time: the computer system's response time is the amount of time it takes from the moment users initiate an activity until the computer begins to present results on the display or printer. [Shneiderman 1998]

Soft real-time systems: systems that can still be considered successful, that is, perform their mission, despite missing some constraints[83].

Software quality assurance: the planned systematic pattern of all

---

[83] There is a continuum between hardness and softness (see definition above) and most systems fit somewhere in between. In a highly simplified form and keeping important exceptions in mind, one can say that most of the systems interacting with human beings use to be soft, while interaction with hardware implies hard timing requirements. There are also cases in which the system puts hard or firm timing requirements on the user.

actions necessary to provide adequate confidence to the system, or process by which the system that is developed conforms to established requirements.

Statistical process control: the application of statistical techniques for measuring, analyzing or controlling the variation in process.

Validation: is the correct system being built? Measurements validation ensures that the metrics reflect the actual requirements.

Verification: is the system being built correctly? Metrics verification ensures that the actual data collected and reported for a metric is accurate.

Appendix B: Erlang

Erlang is a declarative programming language for programming concurrent and distributed, large, real-time systems. Erlang was developed by Ericsson and Ellemtel Computer Science Laboratories. Originally, Erlang was developed for telecommunication switching systems where features from functional and logical languages were combined. Since Erlang provides mechanisms for concurrency, error recovery, fault tolerance and distribution, it is suited for programming many different sorts of embedded, real-time control systems, not only telephone switches.

Erlang programs are known for their short code, efficiency and ease of design, modeling, implementation and maintenance. Due to their mathematical nature, functional programming languages are very well suited for use in the expression of designs. Use of Erlang in a number of different projects has dramatically shortened the time to market and greatly improved the quality of the delivered software.

Erlang consists of the Erlang language and a run-time environment. For an excellent and complete reading on Erlang, see [Armstrong, Virdin, Wikstrom, Williams], a textbook written by the inventors themselves.

Language characteristics

Main features included in Erlang, such as real-time, fault tolerance and distribution mechanisms are presented below.

On code syntax

Applications written in Erlang are divided into modules. Modules are composed of functions and each function consists of clauses. Functions are either only visible inside a module or exported, i.e., they can also be called by functions in other modules. Polymorphism is supported in the sense that different functions can have the same names as long as they have a different number of arguments or different argument data types or exist in different modules. A guard can be specified with a function and means that a certain condition has to be met before evaluating the function body. Conditional evaluation inside a function can be accomplished with a case or an if statement.

Variables in Erlang must start with a capital letter and are assign-once variables. This means that once a variable has been assigned a certain value the variable can never change again. This approach makes careless mistakes less frequent. Apart from the basic data types, Erlang also provides tuples[84] and lists[85]. The language has strict evaluation, which means every part of an expression is calculated even when it is not necessary. Erlang is weakly typed and types are determined dynamically at run-time. Neither global variables nor pointers exist in Erlang. Local or temporary variables are assigned inside functions.

Repeat constructs such as loops do not exist in Erlang. This mechanism is accomplished by recursion.

The work in the system is done by lightweight processes, i.e. processes require little memory and creating processes, deleting processes and message passing require little computational effort. The processes communicate with each other by asynchronous message passing with message queues for each process. Messages are processed from the queue using standard functional language pattern matching semantics. The processes are created dynamically and each process has its own memory which grows and shrinks dynamically.

Real-time

The Erlang systems have an inbuilt notion of time - the programmer can specify how long a process should wait for a message before taking some action. This allows the programming of real-time applications. Erlang is suitable for most soft real-time applications where response times are in order of milliseconds.

While programming in Erlang, it is possible to change the code of a running program, allowing so called "continuous operation". This

---

84 A tuple: a sequence of elements separated by a semicolon. In most cases the elements are grouped within a paranthesis.
85 A list: a sequence of elements separated by a comma. In contrast to a tuple, ordering of the elements is essential and elements may relate to one another.

feature is critical for real-time systems that are impossible to stop for maintenance. In embedded systems, all code is usually loaded at boot time. In development systems, code is loaded as it is needed.

Erlang is a symbolic language with a real-time garbage collector and process scheduler. The process scheduler uses time slicing which means that each process is dedicated a short time fraction. Thus, no process is allowed to block the system.

The Erlang programmer can specify which activities are to be represented as parallel processes. Scheduling is done by grouping the processes and arranging them in a tree.

Erlang has mechanisms for allowing processes to time out while waiting for events and to read a real-time clock.

Erlang is sufficiently fast for delivering real-time telecommunication programs.

Fault-tolerance

Run-time error detection and handling mechanisms allow the construction of robust software. Erlang has mechanisms for:
- Monitoring the evaluation of an expression.
- Monitoring the behaviour of other processes.
- Trapping evaluation of undefined functions.

It is possible to restart only the faulty parts of the program. Processes can monitor each other's behaviour. During execution, processes can establish links to other processes and ports. Ports provide the basic mechanism for communication with the external world and make processes outside Erlang behave as if they were Erlang processes. All process links are bidirectional.

Distribution

The language has built-in mechanisms for distributed programming which makes it easy to write applications which can run either on a

single computer or on a network of computers. All concurrency and error detection primitives have the same properties in a distributed system as in a single node system. Erlang has no shared memory, as all interaction between processes is based on the asynchronous message passing. The distribution characteristics result in:
- Increased speed. The application is split up into different parts which can be evaluated in parallel on different nodes.
- Increased reliability and fault tolerance. The failure of one or more nodes does not affect the system as a whole.
- Extendibility. A system can be designed so that additional nodes can be added in order to increase the capacity of the system. If the system is too slow, one can improve performance by supplying it with more nodes.
- Scalability, as defined in terms of number of users, is improved due to the above effects.

A node is a central concept in distributed Erlang. The term node means an executing Erlang system which can take part in distributed transactions. In a distributed network, one or more Erlang nodes may run on a single computer.

Inter-processor communication makes use of a sophisticated caching technique which makes data transfer highly efficient. A cross-processor remote procedure call in Erlang is often more efficient that in a language such as C [Armstrong 1996]. It is not possible to differentiate between node failures and network failures.

Integration

Erlang can easily make use of programs written in other programming languages. These can be interfaced to a system in such a way that they appear to the programmer as if they were written in Erlang.

Run-time environment characteristics

During the program execution, the code is interpreted by a virtual machine, making Erlang applications platform independent. As a result, a distributed application can be run on a network of different types of machines as long as the appropriate run-time environment is installed on all hosts.

Garbage collecting is done in real time. Memory is allocated automatically when required and deallocated when no longer needed. Typical programming errors associated with memory management can not occur. In implementing large control systems, conventional language problems of memory leakage and fragmentation are extremely difficult to eliminate. The cost of ad hoc solutions outweighs that of using a purpose-built garbage collector. Run-time dynamic memory requirements of a real-time system programmed in Erlang are surprisingly small [Armstrong 1996].

Last call optimization is used to allow recursive functions to be evaluated in constant space.

OTP - Open Telecom Platform

The Erlang Open Telecom Platform (OTP) is designed for development of telecommunication applications. The purpose of OTP is to reduce the time-to-market. Figure B.1 illustrates the OTP system architecture.

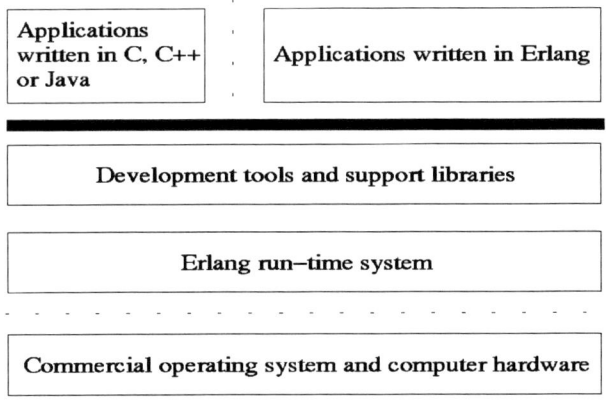

Figure B.1: The OTP system architecture

The system consists of three layers:

- The bottom layer: commercial operating systems and hardware.
- The middle layer: support for telecommunication.
- The top layer: applications.

In addition, the architecture provides three interfaces:
- The interface to the OTP software.
- The interface to the operating system.
- The interface between applications written in different languages.

Among other things, OTP provides the following set of tools and building blocks:
- Applications. The building block of a system. Application hides internal details and provides functionality only through specified interfaces. Most of the time, an application is written as a supervision tree (see below).
- Erlang. The programming language, the compiler[86], the debugger and the virtual machine.
- SASL. The System Architecture Support Libraries contain the necessary functionality for building fault-tolerant and distributed systems.
- Behaviours. Formalizations of design patterns that can be used to build new applications.
- Mnesia. A real-time fault-tolerant distributed database management system.
- SNMP. Simple Network Management Protocol
- Appmon. A program for application monitoring.
- C interface generator. A tool for creating necessary stubs for communication between C and Erlang.
- Coverage tester. Makes sure that all code in a module has been executed.
- Cross-reference tool. A tool for building graphs and find out module dependencies.
- Erlang mode and Emacs. Helps the programmer by providing syntax highlighting and code formatting.
- Profiler. A tool used to detect "hot spots" in the code.
- Kernel. An application that is running at all times. The Kernel provides facilities like authorization, error logging, etc.

---

86 The compiler produces platform independent byte code.

- OS monitoring. Services for controlling available disk space and free memory.
- Sockets. Interface to communication protocols.
- Supervision tree. A process which supervises other processes called children.

OTP supports requirements like robustness, smooth software upgrades, minimized maintenance, distribution and real-time functionality.

Fault-tolerance and reliability in Erlang

Erlang messages are not guaranteed to be delivered. As a result, one can choose to not recover the lost messages or to use one of the numerous techniques of dealing with unreliable communication.

To not recover a message may be desirable in a number of cases:
- When the lost messages have so short a useful lifetime that losing data may be less harmful than getting delayed data.
- When the lost message due to its nature is not critical for continued system operation and may be disregarded.
- When the message contents can be regenerated more easily than recovered.
- When correct timing of the successfully delivered messages is more critical than delivery of all messages, as embedded recovery mechanisms may cause general delays.

Two main families of techniques for error correction are available:
- Backward error correction. This is a family of techniques that are used to recover data after an error in the data has been discovered. The basic mechanism used in these techniques is to retransmit data after it has been determined that an error has occurred in the transmitted data.
- Forward error correction. This is a family of techniques that are used to recover data when errors occur. Unlike backward error correction these techniques do not wait for an error to be discovered. Instead, additional redundant information is transmitted with the data. The redundant information is used to reconstruct the data if it is corrupted or lost.

The functional nature of Erlang provides the system tester with the advantage of being able to test functions individually. Furthermore, if functions have a functional behaviour they can be used with other functions and result in a known outcome.

Erlang provides mechanisms for fault tolerance achievement by static and dynamic redundancy. For a detailed description of techniques and tools, see [Castro 1998] pp. 107-122.

Appendix C: Interview with Mr. Thorleiv Knutsen, WesternGeco, Central Acquisition Systems, 14. March 2002.

WesternGeco, the world's largest seismic company, provides comprehensive worldwide reservoir imaging, monitoring, and development services, with the most extensive seismic crews and data processing centers in the industry, as well as the world's largest multiclient seismic library. Services range from 3D and time-lapse (4D) seismic surveys to multicomponent surveys for delineating prospects and reservoir management.

A dialog has been established between the author and the company and a presentation of the thesis' main achievements and objectives given. A general introduction into the company's major areas of involvement and main product characteristics has been given by the company, as well as a an overall feedback to the presented achievements of the thesis.

Dependability

1. How would you define typical dependability (functional and non-functional) requirements on your systems? Do you have a policy for deriving formal definitions and carrying them though the development stages?

The following top-level attributes are meant by dependability requirements: Correctness, Reliability, Scalability, Efficiency, Security, Safety, Usability, Testability, Flexibility, Maintainability, Portability, Reusability, Interoperability and Evolvability.

Each one of them is relevant during certain development stages and they are quantified by ratings. A level below are criteria and the related metrics.

Dependability level means the level of fulfillment of the dependability requirements. If one attribute is more important than another, please specify how and to what degree, as compared to the overall attributes.

I would look at dependability on two levels:

- *The systems up-time requirements (i.e. the system will guarantee some up-time).*
- *The systems ability to give warnings/alarms when it is not able to perform some task or a group of tasks.*

We have no formal approach to dependability requirements. They will typically be of the nature ("good enough").

2. How do you define integrity requirements on the systems and to what degree are they present? Integrity can be interpreted as consistency and completeness on the different levels: system, component, data, service...

System integrity is somewhat similar to dependability, but I would look at the way it handles its information. An example could be how it handles its state when a part of the system goes down. Assuming this is a valid definition, I would argue that in our case the will be many such requirements. As we are talking of distributed systems it is important to have some opinion as to how the total system should behave in case of loss of some of its resources.

3. What are examples of such (dependability and integrity) requirements, if any?

See 2.
There are other types of requirements as well:
- *Should some backup of system data/state be done?*
- *Should we require that the system actively tries to regain the resource or should it passively wait for the resource to re-appear?*

4. To what degree are these requirements defined during requirements specifications and do they change under operation? Are the requirements set by the customer or are they limited by technically boundaries?

These types of requirements are generally defined at some stage in the requirement specification phase, but in real life they will often be non-measurable statements such as "good enough, well-behaved, user-friendly, adaptive++++".

*Design Guidelines for a Monitoring Environment Concerning
Distributed Real-Time Systems*

The requirements will live its own life, but in general requirements tends to be better and better formalized as the development cycle progresses. Often the first test of the system will come up with refined and additional requirements.

*It is to a large extent the provider of the equipment that sets the requirement (i.e. us), but they are typically based on knowledge on what kind of behavior is required in order to not distort the data in any way (Seismic data has its main information content in below 200Hz, typical sample rate is 2ms (i.e. Nyquist of
250 Hz)). Using these numbers we can know in most cases where the requirement for a certain behaviour is.*

5. How is fulfillment of the requirements ensured under the project development stages and are there connections between assurance policies during the different stages?

Fulfillment of requirements are ensured by the following:
- *Iterative development (i.e. a runnable system is verified every approx. 8 weeks).*
- *Integration test (before system is tried in field).*
- *Alpha Test (an engineering led test under field conditions).*
- *Beta Test (an operations led test leading to a commercialization of the product).*

6. Are you required to be able to measure and guarantee for fulfillment of certain critical requirements?

Typically no. But external customer, may require certain proofs of the behaviour of the system. This is typically done in a lab environment. In addition there will be certain operation requirements that needs to be proven before a set of seismic data produced is accepted by the customer. This is typicall related to the quality of the data itself.

7. How are they measured and guaranteed, in case?

We have operators that produce views/reports of certain

characteristics of the data.

8. Are there examples of costs of requirement breaches?

The cost of not delivering known quality data can be tremendously high. There are quite a high cost in producing data that later proves unusable (run a vessel with 40-50 people wasting their time). An additional cost is if the vessel have left the area where the data is produced before errors in the data is discovered.

9. How is traceability enabled? (Definitions, metrics, design measures, etc.?)

Traceability is typically achieved thorough a collection of logs, produced by various sub-systems. They are typically different in nature from sub-system to sub-system. In reality it is many times harder to claim that we can trace events that have occurred.

10. What methods and techniques do you typically use to fulfill dependability requirements? (Examples can include: redundancy, self-check, analytical methods, voting, exception handling, N-version programming, recovery blocks, software audits, etc.)

The most common method is to use low coupling between components and sub-systems. That way it is easier to guarantee some predicatble behaviour when resources disappears/reappears.
Of the other methods you mention, the most common is redundancy and exception handling.

11. How do you collect and reuse knowledge and experience from old to new, similar projects? Are there any formal methods?

This is to 95% achieved by having people stay extended periods in projects (i.e. a person will belong to a project group producing many generations of a sub-system).

In addition, we have various formal and informal ways to share knowledge between projects and development sites. I.e. no formal methods for transfer of knowledge from one project to another.

Real-time

12. What are the most common real-time requirements on your systems and how are these fulfilled?

The most common real-time requirement is response time (i.e. some piece of hardware or software must take appropriate action within a certain time). The method to deal with these requirements are typically to avoid them (i.e. move real-time behavior lower and lower in the multi-layered designs we are using now (a good example is to look at the shot-awareness (when shot is fired and when it ends. In eralier systems this awareness was spread in all layers, top to bottom, but in the latest designs this awarenes is only on the highest level, implying that we have removed many real-time behaviour requirements from the middle and top layers (using time tagging of events)).

To achieve this smaller and smaller pieces of equipment is system time aware and can therefore time-tag the events it wants some other part of the system to know about.

13. Do these requirements vary over periods of time and how predictable is the target systems behaviour?

Yes, there is quite a bit of consistency requirements, both in terms of system behaviour, but also in terms of data quality. As the target system is a semi-random collection of sub-systems I would argue that the systems behaviour is not very predictable, but that the sub-systems behaviour is.

14. What adjustments/control measures can be made to enhance real-time properties of the system (including both the monitoring environment and the target system) ?

The most realistic approach here, I think, is to look at the complete operation (operators and the equipment)as the system and then I would argue that what could be a cost-effective improvement would be to have a monitoring philosophy that was aimed at suggesting appropriate actions to the operator based on the monitored behaviour. I do not see that our system is predictable enough to actually take action on.

15. What are the main criteria for fulfillment of the real-time requirements and how can these be measured?

This one is a hard one to describe. Basically the sub-system I am working on has this task, and we are basically trying to verify that timing and positions are correct based on measurements of events in the data recorded. I do not think I will be able to answer much more on this one.

16. Are real-time database services embedded into the systems? What issues does this impose?

Yes, but up to now the real-time requirements for database access and information flow has mainly been geared at visualization needs by the operators. More and more the actual system behaviour is dependent on real-time requirements for the data bases used. The issues it typically raises is related to performance. It often enforces a very shallow database model to optimize access times+++.

Distributed systems

17. What issues does distribution impose?

Quite a few I would say:
- *Try to distribute with as low coupling and as much one-way dependencies as possible (i.e. avoid two-way dependencies).*
- *Understand the synchronous/asynchronous behaviour you need (choose asynchronous if possible).*

Communication libraries such as IP, UDP, TCP, CORBA, RMI, DCOM is not guaranteed, but deliver a good average performace. Design with this in mind.
++++

18. How are these handled?

I have described some techniques under 18, but there are more.

Design and monitoring

19. What do you see as the main design-related drawbacks of your systems in terms of error sources and how do you classify them? What is their respective severity?

As it is today, I would say the mix of control and GUI functionality in the same process is maybe the biggest problem.

In addition, the system shares resources with the user and this also poses grat challenges when trying to guarantee some deterministic behaviour from the system.

20. What preventative measures have been designed for error occurrences? To what degree does design ensure fulfillment of dependability requirements?

I can say something about how we are thinking now:
- *Design with simple components (doing one task and beeing good at that one task).*
- *Use store first pattern (i.e. do not rely on information before you have stored it (important as data volumes are high and we want some functionality to run even if there are errors in other parts))*
- *Complete separation between presentation, control and storage layers.*
- *Use commercial products for general functionality (i.e. communication protocols, GUI libraries, databases+++).*

21. Are the systems monitored, how and what functions does the monitoring have?

Well, the whole system is a monitoring system, but as of today it performs its monitoring tasks by providing visual feedback to a user.

Design Guidelines for a Monitoring Environment Concerning Distributed Real-Time Systems

The purpose of the system is to quality control equipment, operation of other systems and the data the other systems are collecting.

22. To what degree is monitoring expected to increase and control the dependability?

I would say to a low degree. It is more likely that the system evolves into a monitoring system able to provide corrective suggestions to the user.

23. What kind of a monitoring environment do you consider as being optimal for the system?

Optimal: monitoring tool cabpable to take preventive actions.
Realistic: As described under 22.

24. How adaptable are your systems to environment and requirements changes in terms of both functional and non-functional requirements?

I would argue that the version we are working on now will be very flexible as we are building the system based on many highly independent components. There will be limitations to the non-functional requirements, but most can be met through the highly distributed nature of the architecture.

25. Can measurements, preventative actions and changes on the system(s) be performed in real-time?

As the systems behaviour is of such a complexity, the most likely goal for us would be to have suggestions for user actions to be taken. I.e. not to take actions on the system directly.

26. How does the choice of overall software and hardware solutions contribute to the dependability achievement and maintenance?

There are many ways we achieve this. A good example is that we select the same platform (Sun-Solaris) on most of our sub-systems. That way we can exploit user skills across sub-system boundaries. The same philosophy is used on software technology. Similar solutions are spread across our products, to make their behaviour seem more similar to the user than they actually are. Even for the software architecture and software tools/libraries this philosophy is used.

The developed monitoring framework

27. Does the presented framework have a business case in your opinion and what is in case its potential?

It is hard to give a straight answer to this, but I would argue that the knowledge gathering and analysis part of the presented framework could be utilized. Even this is hard to achieve as the total system changes in "random" steps (i.e. various sub-systems change independent of each other).

28. Do you know about existing comparable intelligent applications for dependability control or requirement frameworks in general?

In fact, many of our applications are trying to achieve some parts of this, but they are not built around a single design concept so you will find varying degree of intelligence in the sub-systems. Remember that most of our sub-systems have a monitoring and control functionality built within the system.

29. To what degree is the presented monitoring environment architecture needed and beneficial?

I would argue that to exploit the potential benefits of the presented monitoring architecture, we would have to enforce more hierarchical planning and control in our design effort. Today the various sub-systems are developed highly independent of each other. However, I think many of the ideas in the presented architecture may be useful to add/use on the sub-system level as these are typically controlled by a single organizational unit.

30. Is the concept technically realistic due to its high efficiency

requirements, volumes and complexity?

I think for us it would be realistic to a have the knowledge learning and analysis part included, but probably not the decision making part.

31. Do you have suggestions on adjustments of the design, methodologies or techniques?

I would say that you should try to formalize the boundaries between:
- *Knowledge Gathering*
- *Knowledge analysis*
- *Suggestions based on the analysis*
- *Actions taken based on the analysis*

32. Can an implementation be cost-beneficially justified and would it require preliminary adjustments (such as constraints to only partial implementation, assumptions, pre-analysis, integration with existing functionalities, etc.)?

Refer to earlier answers. (knowledge gathering, analysis and suggestions probably yes).

33. What should be done to introduce the concept or parts of it to already existing systems?

We have an information management system today, and it seems to me that some of the ideas might be utilized within this sub-system. They are today trying to introduce hierarchical reporting of state information of the various sub-systems).

34. How would your systems and organization in general benefit from such a concept?

Mostly on an architecture and design philosophy level. As sub-systems are developed quite independently in our case, the way we change is more based on the design thinking patterns rather than strict enforcement of design rules.

Costs and benefits

35. What do you see as the main costs and benefits of the dependability framework? How is the trade-off between the different requirements made in your systems?

Main cost: Would probably require organizational change.
Main benefit: Would formalize some of the efforts we already make.